# Science Concept Cartoons®

Revised Edition

Stuart Naylor and Brenda Keogh

**Millgate House Education**

Sponsored and supported by

GlaxoSmithKline

ROYAL SOCIETY
OF CHEMISTRY

The **Association**
for **Science Education**
Promoting Excellence in Science Teaching and Learning

**EPSRC**
Engineering and Physical Sciences
Research Council

First published in 2010 by Millgate House Publishers

Millgate House Publishers is an imprint of
Millgate House Education Ltd.
Unit 1, Zan Business Park
Crewe Road
Sandbach
Cheshire
CW11 4QD
UK

www.millgatehouse.co.uk

Copyright © Millgate House Education 2014

*British Library Cataloguing in Publication Data*
A catalogue record for this book is available from the British Library.

ISBN  978-0-9562646-4-0

Graphic design by Bill Corrigan & Neil Pepper
Illustrations by Ged Mitchell

Printed and bound in Great Britain by Cambrian Printers

# Contents

# i. Acknowledgements
## and preface to the Second Edition

This book was initially developed as a part of the Concept Cartoons in Science Education Project, which aims to improve classroom practice in teaching, learning and assessment in science education. The project was made possible by the support of a number of individuals and organisations.

We wish to express our grateful thanks to:
- our sponsors, for enabling teachers and pupils to have access to the book, namely GlaxoWellcome plc, Association for Science Education, Engineering and Physical Sciences Research Council, Institute of Physics, Particle Physics and Astronomy Research Council, Royal Society of Chemistry and SCIcentre
- Catherine Wilson, Kay Roberts and the late Frank Ellis, for believing in our work and offering endless support
- Alan Goodwin and Jo Moules for their ideas and insight, which helped to clarify our own thinking in generating the background text
- colleagues, teachers and learners of all ages for providing the inspiration for the Concept Cartoons
- our magicians, Ged Mitchell (landscape artist and book illustrator), and Neil Pepper and Bill Corrigan (graphic designers), for sharing our vision of what this book should be and for breathing life into our Concept Cartoons.

In the 10 years since we wrote the first edition we have developed a better understanding of what type of background text is most helpful. You will find that the background text is more precise and focused, and that the language used is now suitable for learners. The background text is for teachers too, but writing it to learners opens up more possibilities of using the text directly with them.

Rewriting the text also makes us realise how much we have learnt during that period. Researching, developing and teaching with Concept Cartoons have been a powerful learning experience for us. We hope that they have a similar impact on you and your learners. If you do find any errors or omissions, please feel free to contact us. Understanding science has many levels, and, like all learners, our understanding is inevitably far from complete.

Brenda Keogh and Stuart Naylor

# ii.   Essential Information

Each section of the book and CD ROM has support material, with ideas for follow up activities and background scientific ideas, written in accessible language. Yes, we do give some possible answers!

Concept Cartoons are normally used near the start of the lesson, followed by paired or small group discussion, and then an opportunity to explore or research the ideas being discussed. You do not need long periods of discussion to have an impact on the lesson.

Ask learners to discuss why each character in the Concept Cartoon might hold their particular idea. What might go in the blank speech bubble? If learners are not confident in expressing their ideas, you might ask them to write their thoughts down first before sharing them.

Some Concept Cartoons may initially appear too easy for some learners, but they can provide a useful starting point for discussion about more challenging concepts and often reveal some basic misunderstandings. They can also be used successfully with older learners who lack confidence in science. If you have the CD ROM you can adjust the level of demand by changing the text.

Avoid being judgemental when learners are sharing their ideas, as this will close down debate and minimise the development of new ideas and understanding. The uncertainty created by the Concept Cartoons is productive.

The main body of the lesson should provide an opportunity for learners to explore, challenge or consolidate the ideas raised through the Concept Cartoon(s). Allow time at the end of the lesson to share ideas and to consolidate learning. Have they changed their minds and why? Do they want to add new ideas to the Concept Cartoon?

Learners can create their own Concept Cartoons as a way of assessing and reviewing their current understanding.

If you want to know more about Concept Cartoons, and how they are used, please visit:

www.conceptcartoons.com

The Concept Cartoons in this book are also available on an interactive CD ROM. More about using the CD ROM is available on the following page.

# Using Concept Cartoons

Science Concept Cartoons Set 1 CD ROM (available separately)

The CD ROM contains all the Concept Cartoons plus ideas for follow up and background scientific ideas, written in accessible language. The speech bubbles on the CD ROM are fully writable.

**Remember to print out any new Concept Cartoons that you create.**

**Using the features on the CD ROM**

The writable speech bubbles enable you to:
·        ask confident pupils what they think the other characters might be saying
·        add learners' ideas to those in the Concept Cartoon
·        keep a printed record of learners' ideas
·        create new Concept Cartoons
·        encourage learners to create their own Concept Cartoons for other groups.

The follow up activities enable you to:
·        share ways of exploring ideas with pupils
·        provide more challenges related to the concept being explored
·        encourage some learners to work independently.

The background ideas enable you to:
·        encourage learners to think about why the characters hold the alternative ideas
·        share solutions to the problem with your learners
·        provide more challenges related to the concept being explored
·        encourage some learners to work independently.

Any Concept Cartoons created by using this software are for use by the purchasing organisation **only and must not be given, or sold, to other individuals or organisations without prior permission from Millgate House Education.**

Essential Information

# iii. Background Information

## What are Concept Cartoons?

'Concept Cartoons are cartoon-style
drawings that put forward a
range of viewpoints about the
science involved in everyday situations.'

They are designed to intrigue, to provoke discussion and to stimulate scientific thinking. By offering different ways of looking at a situation, Concept Cartoons make concepts problematic and provide a stimulus for developing ideas further. They do not always have a single right answer. The outcome may depend on circumstances, definitions and contextual factors. Although some parallels can be found in the research literature, we believe that Concept Cartoons are a unique approach to teaching, learning and assessment.

Our research (Keogh and Naylor, 1999) identifies a number of features that help to make Concept Cartoons effective. These include:

· visual representation of ideas

· minimal text, in dialogue form

· using familiar situations

· offering alternative viewpoints, including the most scientifically acceptable idea(s)

· common areas of misunderstanding, drawn from research and professional practice

· giving the alternatives equal status.

# How are Concept Cartoons used?

Concept Cartoons are used in a variety of ways and in a wide range of settings. The most common reasons for using them are:

- making the learners' ideas explicit
- challenging and developing the learners' ideas
- illustrating alternative viewpoints
- providing a stimulus for discussion and argument
- promoting thinking and reasoning
- helping learners to ask their own questions
- providing starting points for scientific investigation and enquiry
- creating a sense of purpose for the rest of the lesson
- promoting involvement and enhancing motivation
- posing open ended problems
- as extension or consolidation activities
- as a summary of a topic or for revision
- outside lesson time (e.g. homework).

> 'Concept Cartoons are often used at the start of a lesson
> or topic as a stimulus for discussion, to identify areas of
> uncertainty and to suggest questions to be answered.'

Concept Cartoons are generally used to start the learning process, but they can be used partway through, or at the end of, a lesson or topic, where the emphasis is on consolidating learning and applying learning in a new situation. A short period of individual reflection on a Concept Cartoon before discussion starts can be useful for clarifying ideas; similarly some individual follow up after discussion and/or enquiry can be useful for consolidating learning.

> 'Teachers and student teachers also use Concept Cartoons
> for developing their own subject knowledge, by asking questions
> that they may not have thought of asking themselves.'

Research shows that many of the misconceptions held by children are retained into adulthood if they are left unchallenged. So as well as identifying the misconceptions and uncertainties that learners may have, teachers can use Concept Cartoons as a mechanism to review their own understanding, identifying their own uncertainties, and ensure that they can justify which alternatives are correct.

'In each Concept Cartoon on the CD ROM, all the speech bubbles and some of the central text are writable, to enable teachers and learners to create their own Concept Cartoons. The blank speech bubble allows learners to add their own ideas.'

The writable bubbles allow learners to add ideas and to include the mistakes that they think other people might make. Learners can create their own Concept Cartoons to illustrate possible areas of confusion in a topic. Teachers can alter the Concept Cartoons to change the level of demand, or explore new concepts in the same situation.

# Concept Cartoons and talk

Several features of Concept Cartoons help to promote talk between learners:
- The visual stimulus which, for many learners, is more engaging than a written or verbal stimulus
- The limited amount of text, which makes them especially suitable for learners with poor literacy skills
- The cartoon-style format and everyday setting give a strong message of familiarity, making the situations seem accessible
- Presenting ideas in deceptively simple situations promotes engagement with those ideas
- The dialogue between the characters seems to draw learners into their conversation, almost as though the learners are participating in their debate.

Although Concept Cartoons can be used individually, the interaction between learners is important.

The value of encouraging learners to argue about their ideas is becoming more widely recognised in schools. Teachers may have some concerns about managing this interaction, but using Concept Cartoons enables argument to take place in a controlled and purposeful way. Concept Cartoons provide a focus, a context and a purpose for discussion, and they legitimise argument between learners. This kind of talk makes learning better (Alexander, 2006). Having to justify one's ideas to other learners in the group is a powerful mechanism for developing deeper understanding.

> Using Concept Cartoons helps learners who lack confidence
> to share their ideas.

Having different characters putting forward the various alternatives helps to raise the status of each of the alternatives. The threat to a learner's self-esteem from putting forward incorrect ideas is therefore reduced. Having voices speaking for them helps to engage learners who may be reluctant to put forward their own ideas in case they are wrong. After all, if they are wrong then they can blame the cartoon character for putting forward that idea!

# Concept Cartoons and Learning

> 'The potential of generating cognitive conflict means that
> Concept Cartoons can be useful for all learners including those who already
> appear to understand the science involved in the situation.'

All of the alternatives in each of the Concept Cartoons are of equal status. There are no contextual clues, such as facial expressions or one character always having the best understanding, so all the learners are likely to experience cognitive conflict and find that their ideas are challenged. Engagement with a Concept Cartoon can lead to clarification of ideas, more secure learning, and translation of knowledge into deeper understanding. One useful approach is to invite learners to work out why each of the characters might think that their idea is correct.

Using Concept Cartoons has implications for the role of teachers and learners in the classroom. In most classrooms, learners put forward ideas and the teacher evaluates them. However, with Concept Cartoons alternative ideas are presented to the learners and they adjudicate between the alternatives. This is a fairly fundamental shift in role.

> 'Even though the teacher has the overall responsibility for managing
> learning, Concept Cartoons give learners more responsibility
> in the process and the value of their active involvement is enhanced.'

One very significant aspect of Concept Cartoons is motivation. As teachers we know that motivated learners are effective learners, and that if learners are disaffected or alienated, then there is often little real learning taking place. In our experience, teachers using Concept Cartoons consistently find that their pupils are more motivated and engaged.

# Concept Cartoons, Assessment and Learning

'Concept Cartoons help to put the principles of
assessment for learning into practice.'

Concept Cartoons can be used for individual summative assessment. However they are probably more valuable as an assessment for learning tool, in which assessment makes learning more effective (Black and Wiliam, 1998; Black et al, 2002; Black and Harrison, 2004). As learners make their ideas public, the teacher is able to make informal judgements about their ideas. It quickly becomes apparent whether learners have a good grasp of the basic concepts involved, are struggling to make sense of the situation or hold firmly held but misguided beliefs. The teacher can then take these ideas into account to give a sense of purpose and direction to the lesson.

Meanwhile learners have the opportunity to discuss their ideas and to become more aware of what they and their peers think. Concept Cartoons encourage vigorous discussion and debate, and sometimes this can be enough to change a learner's ideas. More frequently, the discussion raises the need for further investigation or research and begins the process of developing the learner's ideas. In this way, using Concept Cartoons for assessment provides a starting point for learning.

'Concept Cartoons identify what learners understand, and create the need
for further enquiry and learning to resolve the conflict between ideas.'

The strength of this connection between assessment and learning was brought home to us when a teacher phoned late one evening to discuss a problem that she had:

" *I've been using Concept Cartoons for assessment but I seem to be doing something wrong. When I use the Concept Cartoons I can't stop the children learning. What should I do?* "

We have used the term 'Active Assessment' to describe this connection, in which purposeful, thought-provoking assessment activities become an integral part of the learning process (Naylor, Keogh and Goldsworthy, 2004; Naylor and Keogh, 2007). Concept Cartoons are not the only active learning approach to assessment. White and Gunstone (1992) give excellent descriptions of a range of techniques which can be used in a similar way. However Concept Cartoons are particularly effective at getting learners thinking about their own ideas and how they might need to develop. They promote metacognition — in other words, they help learners to think about their own learning. Even quite young children have commented on how Concept Cartoons make them think about their own ideas and those of other people.

11

> 'The realisation that there can be lots of ways of thinking about a situation can be a powerful incentive to taking other people's ideas seriously.'

## Concept Cartoons and age range

When we first generated Concept Cartoons, we believed that we would need to target them at particular ages. Experience has taught us that this is not necessarily true, and that many of the Concept Cartoons can be suitable for a very wide age range. Some of the Concept Cartoons originally designed for use with young children have been used successfully with older pupils and adult learners; the converse is also true.

> Sometimes learners can tackle a Concept Cartoon at their own level of understanding, and interpret the problems raised in different ways according to their individual starting points.

The same Concept Cartoon may sometimes be used on more than one occasion and still provide a suitable level of challenge. The writable speech bubbles on the CD ROM add to the scope of many of the Concept Cartoons. In the chapters which follow, we have tried to put Concept Cartoons which are less demanding earlier in the sequence for a particular concept. You may disagree with our choice!

# Life processes in animals and plants

1

**1**

Life processes in animals and plants

# 1.1 Seeds in the dark

You can investigate this by trying to grow a range of different seeds in light and dark places to see if the amount of light makes any difference to the way that they begin to grow. Remember seeds need air, moisture and warmth to help them to begin to grow. What happens if you change the amount of light from none to bright light, or provide light in small bursts or continuously?

Most people know that green plants need light to grow. So you might expect that seeds also need light to begin to grow (germinate). This is not correct. Most seeds do not require any light. If they did need light, then seeds would not germinate when they are buried underground. How much light a seed needs depends on what type of plant it is from, and how the plant disperses the seed. Some seeds (tiny seeds such as celery, for example) may need light to break their dormancy. What other factors, such as temperature, might affect the way that seeds start to grow? Do you think these factors will be different for seeds germinating in different habitats? You could make seed packets based on your ideas.

# 1.2 Upside down seeds

You can investigate this by growing different seeds to find out whether the way that they are planted makes any difference to how they grow. Large seeds are easiest to handle. Which ways can you plant them? Remember seeds need air, moisture and warmth to help them to begin to grow. What happens if you let them begin to grow and then turn them over?

Plants in nature always seem to grow the right way up, even though seeds will have landed randomly on the ground. Plant growth is controlled by chemicals that make the shoots always grow upwards or towards the light, and the roots always grow downwards or towards water. It doesn't matter which way up the seeds are when they start to grow. What happens if the source of light is at the side not the top? You could make a poster based on your ideas.

# 1.3 Muscles

You can find out about how muscles work by feeling the muscles in your arms. When muscles contract they feel hard and tight. When they relax they feel soft and more floppy. What happens when you do different activities, like lifting objects or pushing against a wall? Can you work out how muscles can move your arm in different directions? You can make a model using a jointed cardboard arm and pieces of elastic to represent muscles. Try to explain why the model does not work in exactly the same way as muscles.

When we talk about forces we talk about pushes and pulls. If one muscle moves the arm by pulling, you might think that another muscle pushes to move the arm back again. Unfortunately this is completely wrong! Muscles can only pull or relax. They are arranged in pairs, so that one muscle pulls to move the arm in one direction and the other muscle pulls to move the arm in the opposite direction. How do muscles in other parts of the body work? How does exercise affect muscles? You could make a fitness guide based on your ideas.

# 1.4 Headstand

You can investigate this by getting healthy volunteers to do a headstand or handstand. This could be in PE. Make sure this is done safely. Can you see any visible changes in the pattern of blood circulation? Where there is less blood the skin will look pale. If blood is not leaving the head as quickly as usual then the face will go red. What happens to the pulse rate during a headstand or handstand?

Normally, the head is above the heart. This means that the heart must be able to pump blood upwards against gravity. It also means that blood should still get to the feet during a headstand or handstand. However the distance that the blood needs to be pumped upwards to the feet will be greater. The heart will need to work harder to pump the blood this extra distance. The blood may not return from the head as easily as it does normally. What happens when you hold your hands above your head? You could make a model to show how blood pumps round the body.

Life processes in animals and plants

# 1.5 New plants

You can investigate this with parts of different types of plants. Some plants, like blackberries and sedums, seem to root easily. It is worth including these. Check that plants are not poisonous before you use them. Plant flowers and seeds, and pieces of stems and roots, and leave them to see if they grow. How will you make sure that you provide the conditions that they need for growth? Can you spot any differences between the places where new roots and shoots start to grow and where they don't grow? Is it different for different plants?

There is more than one possible answer to this problem depending on the plant. If flowers are planted they rarely grow into a new plant. However seeds, parts of the stem and parts of the root often grow into new plants, although some may take a long time. In some plants (for example, couch grass or willow) almost any piece of stem or root seems able to grow into another plant. There are other plants (for example, annual flowers) that only seem to grow from seeds, so pieces of stem or root usually die. It is difficult to predict precisely what will happen with an individual plant. How do people who propagate plants know which part to use? You could discuss your ideas with a gardener.

# 1.6 Beans

You can investigate this by growing some beans and observing how they turn as they climb. What factors might make a difference? Can you make the beans grow in different directions? What if beans grow upside down? Do different types of beans spiral in different ways? What about other plants that grow in spirals? You can contact schools in other countries to compare how beans grow there. Science Across The World, on the ASE website (www.ase.org.uk) is a good way to make links with schools in other countries.

Beans and other climbing plants (such as vines) usually grow in a spiral, but they might not always grow anti-clockwise. There has been much discussion about this, and a web search will reveal lots of debate. One theory is that some types of plant twist in the same direction wherever they are grown, but other types will twist in either direction depending on how they touch their support. See if you can find Michael Flanders and Donald Swann's amusing song, called Misalliance, that is based on this problem. Can you create your own song?

Life processes in animals and plants

# 1.7 Babies

You can't do a simple practical investigation to find out about this situation. The most useful thing to do is to find out about how animal reproductive systems have evolved. Start with simple animals and move on to more complex animals, such as mammals. Which animals lay eggs? Which animals give birth to live young? Which animals have small numbers of babies? Are there some animals that don't fit the pattern?

There isn't a single reason why humans don't lay eggs. Developing inside the mother is safer and more efficient, so babies can be bigger and more developed when they are born. A human egg would need a very thick eggshell to protect it. This might be a problem for the baby to break through. Animals that lay eggs use different ways to protect them, such as burying them, making nests, and sitting on eggs to protect them. What do you think humans would do if they did lay eggs? How would they protect the eggs? How do you think this might affect human behaviour? You could make a cartoon strip based on your ideas.

Life processes in animals and plants

# 1.8 Small fish

Investigating fish in a pond is not easy. You could investigate what happens with other living things. Plants are easier to grow than animals. What happens if you grow different types of plants with restricted light or nutrients, or grow them in a restricted space? Do any of these affect the growth rate and the final size of the plants? Talk to a fish breeder or do a web search to find out more information about this problem.

There is more than one possible answer to this problem. A group of fish might be small because of their genetic background, because there isn't enough food for them to grow any bigger, because of other environmental factors, or because of a combination of these factors. It isn't possible to give a general answer, but the science behind the growth of fish (and other animals) affects decisions made by people who breed them, and has implications for the animals' welfare. Can you find out more about this and produce a report?

Life processes in animals and plants

# 1.9 Heavy plants

You could investigate this by trying to weigh the soil before and after a period of plant growth to find out if soil is taken up through the roots. What happens if you use other materials to grow plants in, such as cotton wool, paper towels, etc? What if you grow plants in water without soil? Find out what happens if plants do not get air or sunlight. Find out about Van Helmont's willow tree experiment.

It is easy to think that plants feed on soil through their roots in the same way that animals take in food through their mouths. This is not correct. Plants do need nutrients to grow. People talk about feeding the plants when they add nutrients to soil or water to help plant growth. This can be confusing. It may seem surprising that air and water turn into new cells in the plant, but this is what happens. In the process of photosynthesis, carbon dioxide (from the air) and water (from the soil) produce carbohydrates with the aid of light energy. What happens to the carbohydrates once they are produced? How do they support other life?

# 1.10 Pond life

This is difficult to investigate without harming the fish. If you have suitable equipment you can measure the oxygen level in the water to see if the oxygen level changes. If it does change, what might cause the change? Think about how aquatic plants can get carbon dioxide for photosynthesis.

Unless the conditions are very unusual it is unlikely that the fish will use up all the oxygen and die. Fish have been living in ponds for many years without using up all the oxygen and dying, so they must get oxygen from somewhere. The fish will get more oxygen from the air as it dissolves in the water. Carbon dioxide also dissolves in water, and plants use this when they photosynthesise. The plants release oxygen into the water during photosynthesis. This oxygen can be used by the fish. Can you find examples of events that have affected the level of oxygen in water? What caused this, and how could it be prevented? What is the impact on fish and other animals living in the water?

Life processes in animals and plants

# 1.11 Eggs

If you are hatching eggs then you can observe what happens by weighing the eggs regularly and calculating whether and how the weight changes. If you are not hatching eggs you could carry out some research. You could do a thought experiment, using ideas about growth, metabolism, energy and particle theory, to decide what will happen to the weight. What do you already know about these, or what can you find out, that will help your discussion?

The amount of food in the egg is fixed when the egg is laid, so it is unlikely that the egg will get heavier. As the chick grows some of the nutrients are converted to carbon dioxide and water to release energy for growth, and the carbon dioxide can leave the egg through the shell. Therefore the egg should get lighter as the baby chick develops inside the egg. After the chick hatches it begins to feed, and from then on its weight starts to increase. Does the same thing happen with seeds? You can use Concept Cartoon 1.12 to help you to think about this.

# 1.12 Seeds

You can investigate this by weighing seeds regularly and calculating whether and how the weight changes. You need to decide whether to weigh the seeds wet or dry. You can dry the seeds completely at about 95°C, so that the dry weight of the seeds can be measured, but it will also kill the seeds. To take regular measurements of the dry weight, you can weigh samples from a large batch of germinating seeds. This will allow the rest of the seeds to carry on growing. What will happen if seeds grow for long enough for the shoots to turn green and start to photosynthesise?

As the seeds grow some of the nutrients are converted to carbon dioxide and water to release energy for growth, so their dry weight (their weight after drying at 95°C) will decrease. However the seeds can absorb water from the environment, so their weight before drying will increase. As the shoot grows and leaves develop, the seedling will start to photosynthesise. From then on its dry weight will also increase. Does the same thing happen with eggs? You can use Concept Cartoon 1.11 to help you to think about this.

Life processes in animals and plants

# Living things and their environment

2

2

Living things and their environment

# 2.1 Rotting apple

You can investigate how quickly an apple rots by observing what happens if you leave it on the surface of different types of soil and in other places. Where does it rot fastest? Can you find ways to slow down or stop the apple rotting? What happens if you wrap the apple in different materials, such as cling film or cloth, or if you spray it with acid (e.g. lemon juice) or disinfectant? What happens at different temperatures, or if the apple is damp or dry?

**Safety note:** wash your hands if you touch the rotting apple

Some people think that apples rot because bad weather, such as frost or rain, somehow attacks them. In fact apples rot because microbes (microscopic organisms such as bacteria) feed on them. This is hard to observe because microbes are too small to see without a microscope. The amount of moisture, the temperature and other factors such as acidity can affect how quickly the microbes feed on the apple and make it rot. How can you use what you have learnt to help you to decide how to handle food safely and slow down the rate at which it rots?

# 2.2 Worms

You can watch what worms do in newly dug soil or in a wormery. What do they eat and how do they get their food? Are worms sensitive to light? Try shining a light on them and watch how they react. What problems do you think worms will face in living underground? How can their structure and behaviour help them to live successfully underground?

Animals have adaptations that enable them to survive in certain places. Worms are adapted to living underground. This helps them to avoid predators such as birds and avoid drying out. It gives them access to a regular food supply of leaves and other organic material. They can't see in the dark, but they have simple eyes so they know when they are near the soil surface during daylight, to avoid being seen by predators. Which other animals live underground? How do their adaptations help them to survive in this environment? You could create a guide to animals that live underground and how they survive there.

Living things and their environment

# 2.3 Plants and animals

It is difficult to do a practical investigation to solve this problem. Think about what the rabbits eat, and what would happen if they had no food. Then think about what the foxes eat, and what would happen if they had no food. Can you predict what will happen if the plants die?

Green plants are part of nearly all food chains and webs, so without them life on Earth could not continue in the way that we know it. If all the plants died then eventually all the animals would die as well. The first to begin to die out would be the herbivores that eat the plants; then the carnivores, that eat the herbivores, would run out of food as well. Scavengers that live on dead animals would have food for a while, but eventually all of the animals would die. What do you think would happen if the top predators were wiped out? Imagine there has been a huge fire that wiped out all the plants and animals. Can the land support life again? If so, in what sequence would the animals and plants return?

# 2.4 Blackbirds

**What do YOU think?**

You can research blackbirds' habits using the internet. What do blackbirds usually eat? Do they eat caterpillars? What do they feed on during the winter when the ground is frozen and no worms are available? Are they territorial? Do they migrate over long distances? Questions like these will help to guide your research.

Blackbirds have a number of ways of surviving if there is not very much food. The blackbird does not only eat one type of food. If there are not many worms then the birds feed on other food sources. They are more likely to feed on small invertebrates such as spiders and snails, as well as berries and seeds, rather than caterpillars. They may be able to find new territories somewhere else, but all the available territories may be full. What can you find out about the impact of severe weather conditions on animal populations and how they survive?

# 2.5 Compost heap

Leave vegetable scraps to rot in a transparent container without worms and other invertebrates. What happens if you add a small amount of soil or compost? What happens to vegetable scraps placed on the surface of a wormery? What changes do you see? Does the temperature change?

**Safety note:** don't seal the container; don't touch the rotting vegetables; don't use meat, fish, cheese, milk or eggs.

Vegetable scraps on a compost heap don't disappear – they change into compost. These changes occur because the vegetable scraps get eaten and digested. Worms and microbes help this to happen. The process of rotting is caused mainly by microbes that feed on organic material. They break down the vegetable scraps and this creates compost. This also generates heat, which makes the vegetable scraps rot faster. Can you use what you have learnt to plan how to set up a compost heap so that the vegetable scraps help to make good compost?

# 2.6 My cat

Find out more about how animals are put into groups. You can use the internet or books for more information about this. Which animals are grouped together? Do humans go into any of the groups? What about cats and fish? What about other creatures such as spiders? Does each animal go into just one group, or into several groups?

Some people think that all animals have four legs and fur, and that people and fish are not animals. This is not correct. The term 'animal' includes people, cats, fish and lots of other things. The large group of animals is divided into smaller groups. People go into the human, mammal, vertebrate and animal groups. Cats go into the mammal, vertebrate and animal groups. Other creatures such as fish or butterflies are not mammals, but they are animals. Which groups does a tarantula belong to? Understanding more about how animals are grouped helps us to make sense of the definitions. How did the work of a scientist named Linneaus help us to make sense of the animal kingdom? Have these ideas changed since he carried out his work?

Living things and their environment

# 2.7 Pollution

You can use books and the internet to find out what kinds of waste products are produced by vehicles and factories. Make sure you include carbon dioxide and water vapour. Do you think these waste products are likely to cause damage to the environment? What about other things, such as litter and cigarette butts? How might they damage the environment? Discuss your ideas. There are lots of internet websites that will tell you more about the possible environmental damage that waste products could cause.

Pollution involves some kind of damage to the environment. Litter may look unpleasant, but not everyone thinks that it is pollution. This is because most litter does not cause any serious environmental damage. However, some litter (e.g. plastic bags) can be damaging. Concerns are being raised about the impact of the millions of cigarette butts discarded every year. There is a lot of evidence of the environmental damage caused by cars and factories, but less about the effect of people smoking on the environment. Did you find any information about this? How do you think you can help to reduce environmental damage?

# 2.8 Recycling

You can investigate what happens to paper that is left outside for a while. Where would be useful places to try? Don't forget to check it regularly to see whether it breaks down naturally. What do you notice? Does it biodegrade? Can you find out how much energy is required to make new or recycled paper? Is it the same for both? Can you work out the possible consequences of not recycling any paper?

Materials are recycled for several reasons, such as re-using scarce raw materials, reducing the waste products created during manufacturing, and reducing the energy used to make the materials. The main purpose of recycling paper is to reduce the amount of energy used, since less energy is needed to make new paper from scrap paper than from trees. It also reduces the need for land for growing trees for making paper. Some people argue that recycling paper is not energy efficient. Why is this? How much recycling do you do at home and at school? What types of recycled paper do you use in your everyday life? You could create a display of these.

Living things and their environment

# 2.9 Making bread

Discuss what you know about microbes. Use a dictionary to check your ideas. What happens to the ball of dough when you make bread with yeast? What happens when a sugar solution is mixed with some dried yeast? What do yeast cells look like if you look at them through a microscope? Which factors do you think might affect how quickly yeast cells grow? How will you investigate this?

Lots of people think that all microbes are harmful. This is not correct. Yeast is an example of a useful microbe, unlike some others that might cause food to go mouldy or make us ill. Worms and spiders can be seen easily with the naked eye, so they are not microbes. Microscopic yeast cells cause sugar to ferment, and this creates carbon dioxide that makes the dough rise. The best conditions for yeast growth are a warm temperature, neutral pH, and sugars such as sucrose. How does yeast make a difference to your life? What would life be like without it?

# 2.10 Rabbits and foxes

It is difficult to do a practical investigation to solve this problem. You can model population changes in rabbits and foxes, using simple arithmetic or with a computer program, or you can find information on the internet. This will show you how the two populations are likely to interact. See if you can predict how the numbers of each animal might change if you start with different numbers of each.

Several factors affect the population size of any animal. These include how much food is available, how fast they grow, how quickly they reproduce, and how many are eaten by other animals. The reproduction rate of the rabbits needs to be higher than that of the foxes if they are to survive, since lots of the rabbits will be eaten by the foxes. A large rabbit population is needed to support a small fox population. Can you find examples of where populations of animals have become unusually large, such as the plague of mice in Australia? What causes this and what is the impact of these changes?

Living things and their environment

# 2.11 Cactus spines

**What do YOU think?**

What can you find out through investigation? You could try planting cactus spines to see if they grow into new plants. You could try to grow cacti in washed gravel to see if they need soil. Cacti grow really slowly, so if you don't have much time to investigate you can find out through books, internet sources or from someone who grows cacti for a hobby. What can you find out about other plants that live in deserts?

The cactus spines are adapted for life in a harsh environment. Their small area helps to avoid water loss, and their sharp ends help to prevent animals eating the succulent stems. Cactus spines do not normally grow into new plants. Cacti contain chlorophyll and use air, water and sunlight to photosynthesise in the same way that other plants do. Unlike most plants the chlorophyll is in the fleshy stem, not the leaves. How do other plants survive in harsh or unusual environments? You could talk to a grower of cacti about your ideas.

# 2.12 Baby blackbirds

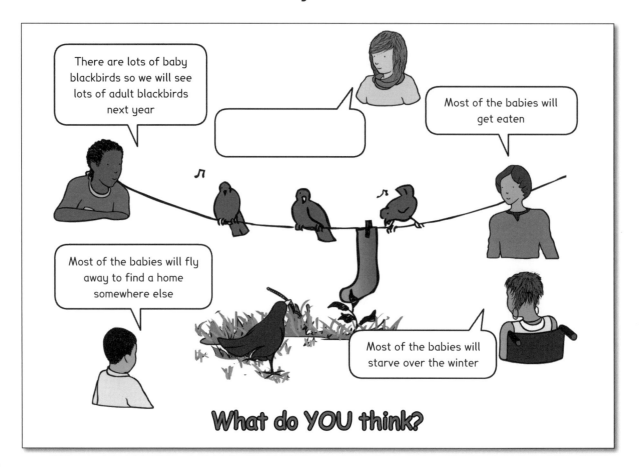

You can't solve this problem by carrying out a simple investigation. You can model population changes using simple arithmetic or with a computer program. What happens if lots of baby blackbirds survive to breed? What happens if hardly any survive to breed? Use books or the internet to find out more about what happens to populations of birds over the winter.

Each pair of animals needs to produce, on average, two offspring that survive to breed in future years. If this doesn't happen then they may die out, or they may increase to unsustainable levels. The blackbird population will vary a bit from year to year. A large number of baby blackbirds may mean that more will get eaten, or that more will starve over the winter. They might be able to find new territories somewhere else, but all the available territories may already be full if there are lots of blackbirds everywhere else. Which animals have the largest number of offspring? Why might that be? Is the number of offspring that animals produce related to the environment where they live? You could use graphs or tables to help you to analyse this information.

Living things and their environment

# The nature of materials

3

41

# 3.1 Balloon

You can investigate this by using very sensitive scales and comparing the difference in how much a balloon weighs before and after it is inflated. You could try to make a lever balance using a long stick or ruler with a blown-up balloon balanced on each end. What do you think will happen when one of the balloons is burst, and the air is released? To let the air out of the balloon gently, stick a piece of Sellotape onto the balloon, then push a pin carefully through the Sellotape. How can you explain what happens?

It is easy to think that air weighs nothing or that it has negative weight. Like all substances, air is made of particles. The particles are very tiny, but they do weigh something. If air does weigh something, then filling the balloon with air will make it heavier. The more air it contains, the more it will weigh. Can you think of any reasons why it is better to use a lever balance than using scales for this investigation?

The nature of materials

# 3.2 Snowman

You can investigate this problem using real snow or ice. Model snowmen can be made by freezing water inside small plastic drinks bottles. What will you use to make a coat? You could use an old glove or sock. How will you measure whether the coat makes any difference? What can you find out about the effect of other factors, such as the fabric, colour and thickness of the coat?

It is easy to think that some materials have the property of making things warm. We put coats on to keep warm, so it is easy to think that the coat will warm the snowman and make it melt quickly. In fact a coat acts as an insulator. It reduces heat transfer in either direction. A coat keeps a person warm but it stops the snowman from getting warmer. The snowman will not melt easily while wearing a coat. Other factors, such as the air temperature and the fabric of the coat, also affect how the snowman melts. How can you use what you have learnt to help you think about how to save money on heating your home?

The nature of materials

# 3.3 Soil

You can try measuring how long it takes for a set amount of water to drain through different types of soil. How much water drains through in a set time? What do the grains of soil look like through a microscope? Does the size of the grains make a difference to how much water drains through the soil? Does all the water drain through each type of soil? What happens if you use wet or dry soils? Does the amount of stones, leaves, twigs, etc. make a difference to how well the soil drains?

How quickly water drains through the soil depends on the size of the air spaces, and the size of the air spaces depends on the size of the grains in the soil. Sand grains are much bigger than grains of clay. This means that the sandy soil will have bigger air spaces and the water will run through more quickly. Other materials in the soil can help to slow down the water movement. This will help the soil retain water and stay wet for longer. What do you think will be the differences between a farm with clay soil and a farm with sandy soil?

# 3.4 Liquids

Careful observation will help you to explore this problem. Would a microscope or hand lens help? What kind of substances can you look at? Choose some that you think are obvious, such as wood and water. Choose some that are not so obvious, such as gel, foam and sand. Are there some things that don't seem to fit with how you would describe a solid, a liquid or a gas?

What is a liquid? Usually we say that the volume of a liquid is fixed but the shape can change. This means that a liquid will take the shape of a container. Modelling clay seems a bit like a liquid. It can have its shape changed, but normally it doesn't change its shape until something changes it. 'Runny solids', such as sand or salt, seem to take on the shape of the container, but they are not liquids. If you look closely at sand or salt you can see tiny grains. These tiny grains do not change shape like liquids do. Each piece is a small solid. Whipped cream is a mixture of liquid and air. It can be runny or thick, depending on the amount of air in it, so it is difficult to categorise. Draw a scale with solids at one end and gases at the other. Where would you put pictures of the substances that you have been exploring?

The nature of materials

# 3.5 Fizzy drink

You can observe what happens to the weight by using a very sensitive balance to weigh the bottle before and after the top is removed to see whether its weight changes. You could use a lever balance too. Put a bottle of fizzy drink on each side and make sure they are balanced. Use a can if it is easier to balance. Now remove the top very carefully to avoid spray or spills. It takes a long time for most of the gas to be lost, so you can reduce evaporation by using a cotton wool plug or cling film. This will help to make your investigation more accurate. How will you decide when all the gas has left the liquid?

It is easy to think that gases weigh nothing or that they have negative weight. When the top is taken off the bottle, carbon dioxide gas will leave. Like all substances, carbon dioxide gas is made of particles. The particles are very tiny, but they do weigh something. Because this gas does weigh something, the fizzy drink will weigh less when the gas has left. Even if some air dissolves in the fizzy drink and replaces some of the carbon dioxide, there will be a weight loss. Can you work out the volume of gas that was in the fizzy drink if 1 gram of carbon dioxide has a volume of about 500 ml?

The nature of materials

# 3.6 Teapot

You can investigate this situation using real teapots full of hot water. Measure the rate of cooling using a thermometer or data logger. What do you think will make a difference to the way that the teapot cools? You can model the situation using different containers full of hot water. This will let you identify the effect of each factor separately.

**Safety note:** the water does not need to be boiling hot. Hot tap water will work. The use of hot water must be supervised by an adult.

How quickly is energy lost from different materials? Energy loss from the teapot will depend on the thickness. A thicker teapot will be a better insulator. The type of material, and how shiny it is, will make a difference. Metals are good conductors of energy, so the metal one will tend to cool down quickly. Also dark colours and dull surfaces lose energy more quickly. The relationship between the different factors is difficult to predict accurately. How does what you have learnt help you to decide which type of teapot to use at home and why tea cosies are used by some people?

The nature of materials

# 3.7 Boiling water

You can investigate this situation by using saucepans or any other suitable container for boiling water. You can compare the time water takes to boil using different amounts of water. You can compare the boiling temperature using different amounts of water. What happens if you heat the water more strongly? Do you think you will get the same result if you compare the boiling time and boiling temperature using other liquids, such as salt solution or milk?

**Safety note:** the use of hot liquids must be supervised by an adult.

It is easy to think that small amounts of liquid will boil at a lower temperature than larger amounts. This is not correct. It takes less energy to boil a smaller amount of liquid so small amounts will boil more quickly. The boiling temperature will be exactly the same in the small and the large pans. Does this make a difference to how you cook vegetables at home?

# 3.8 Submarine

You can investigate how much solids, liquids and gases can be compressed. You need to measure the volume of the material, then put it under pressure (for example, in a large syringe) and then measure the volume again to see if it has changed. Do solids, liquids and gases change by the same amount?

Normally solids and liquids can't be compressed much, but gases can be compressed much more easily. This is because the particles in solids and liquids are very close together, so they can't get much closer. In a gas there are bigger spaces between the particles, so it is possible to squeeze the particles closer together. Can you find examples of when compressed air is used? What do you think will happen to the volume of solids, liquids and gases if you change the temperature?

The nature of materials

# 3.9 When water is boiling

Without complicated equipment it is difficult to find out what the bubbles are made of in boiling water. But you can collect the gas rising from the boiling water. How could you test it to find out whether it is water, hydrogen, oxygen or air? For safety reasons these tests must only be done with adult supervision. Make sure that the water is pure before it is boiled to eliminate any possibility of impurities. What is steam made from? Will it be the same as the bubbles?

We often think that liquids boil at the surface, probably because that is where we see the evidence of boiling. In fact the water boils at the bottom of the pan because that is where it is heated. When the water boils it turns into a gas and this makes the bubbles The bubbles are filled with gaseous water. Although water is made up of hydrogen and oxygen, the hydrogen and oxygen do not split apart. Separating hydrogen and oxygen is a difficult and dangerous process. Can you find out how water can be split into hydrogen and oxygen?

# 3.10 Scrambled egg

Make some scrambled egg and see if the white and yolk can be separated again. Try gently heating the yolk and the white separately, and see what happens to them. Find out what you can about the definition of elements, compounds and mixtures, using books or internet sources. What can you find out about the chemical make up of eggs?

An element is a pure substance containing only one type of atom, a compound has two or more elements combined chemically, and a mixture is two or more elements or compounds mixed together. It is easy to be confused about this problem because eggs are not made from a single pure substance. Eggs are made up of a complex mixture of compounds that are changed chemically during heating. This is an irreversible change. What other irreversible changes can you find in the kitchen?

The nature of materials

# 3.11 Helium balloon

**What do YOU think?**

You can investigate this situation using helium balloons. What happens if you let some of the helium out? What happens if you warm and cool the balloons? How can you measure how well the balloons float? Could you use something light fastened to the balloon (such as a paper clip) to see how much it will lift?

We do not usually think about things floating in air. We are more used to talking about things floating in water. The helium is buoyant compared to air. In other words it weighs less than the same volume of air, so a balloon full of helium will float in air. More helium makes the balloon float better. When the balloon is warmed its volume increases. This means that the same mass of gas fills a bigger volume, so its density decreases and it will float better. The reverse occurs when the balloon goes in a freezer. How does what you have learnt help you to work out how a hot air balloon works?

# 3.12 Mountains

It is difficult to do a practical investigation to explore this problem. You can use reference books and the internet. You can reason from experience. You may be able to think of models or analogies that help to explain what happens. Can you predict what would happen if each of the statements were correct? What can you find out about the atmosphere at different heights above the Earth?

It helps to understand the nature of air particles and where they are. The particles in the air do not change size or shape depending on temperature or altitude, but there are fewer particles in the air at higher altitudes. Although individual particles are moving around randomly at high speeds, they are still attracted to the Earth by the force of gravity, so there will be more air at the bottom of the mountain than the top. This is why the Earth's atmosphere is only present in a relatively narrow band around the Earth's surface. How does what you have learnt help you to explain why mountaineers who climb Everest need to take oxygen with them?

The nature of materials

# Changes in materials

4

Changes in materials

# 4.1 Salty water

You can investigate this by finding out how long it takes for the same amount of salt to dissolve in water at different temperatures. It is harder to find out how much salt dissolves in water, or if salt will dissolve in cold water. You could weigh some salt, then add a little at a time until you see that it has stopped dissolving, then work out how much has dissolved. Can you think of any other ways to find out? What else might make a difference to salt dissolving? What do you think will happen as the water gets colder and starts to freeze?

Salt dissolves faster in hot water than in cold water. Everything is made of small particles, including water. As the temperature increases the particles in the water move faster, so the salt dissolves more quickly. It is easy to think that salt will not dissolve in cold water, but it does. Even in cold water the particles are still moving. Some people live in places where the water is 'hard'. See if you can find out what this means. How does what you have learnt about dissolving help you to explain the problems that people have if they live in an area where water is hard.

Changes in materials

# 4.2 Muddy water

You can compare filters such as cotton wool, a fine sieve, one or more thicknesses of filter paper, and a commercial water filter. Which filter works best? How will you know? What happens if you evaporate the clean water that you have collected? Are there any substances in the water that you can see only when all the water has evaporated?

Filtering will trap stones and soil so that the water looks clean. The better the filter, the more material will be trapped and the cleaner the water will look. However, dissolved substances can pass through a filter, so although the water looks clean it may not be safe to drink. Use what you have learnt to think about the issues that people face if they live in countries where drinking water is not purified.

Changes in materials

# 4.3 Condensation

You can investigate this by observing what happens when you take a cold empty glass out of a freezer and fill it with ice. Does the outside of the glass get wet? If it does, where could the water have come from? Does it happen wherever you put the glass, for example indoors and outdoors? Look at windows in a classroom, or in a car, when people have wet clothing. Look at mirrors in bathrooms, or people's spectacles after they come inside on a very cold day. What do you see, and how can you explain it?

The water we see on glasses and other surfaces is called condensation. We see condensation in lots of different places, but it isn't obvious where the water comes from. There is normally water vapour in the air, but it is a colourless gas so we can't see it. Where the temperature is lower the gas turns into droplets of liquid. This is what we see as mist or condensation. Condensation usually forms when moist air hits a cold surface. A glass containing ice is usually cold enough for water vapour in the air to turn into droplets of liquid water on the side of the glass. Compare the amount of condensation that you get in different places, such as where there is still air, moving air, cold air, warm air, dry air and moist air. What do you notice? Condensation can cause problems in houses. Can you use what you have learnt to think how condensation might be reduced?

# 4.4 Rusting

You can set up a practical investigation to find out what makes nails go rusty. What do you think might make a difference? How will you separate each of the possible factors? Removing air completely is the most difficult. A layer of oil, paint or petroleum jelly will keep the air out, but it also stops moisture getting to the nail. Boiling water for a few minutes will remove the air, so you can do a comparison with a nail with water and no air. Does it make a difference if the water contains salt or other substances? What happens if you use iron, zinc or copper nails?

Iron nails go rusty if air and water are present, so wet nails usually rust fairly quickly. If they are completely underwater they will slowly go rusty, because water normally contains dissolved air. Cold conditions will slow down rusting. In salty water iron tends to rust more quickly. Although rust may look like a disease, it isn't, so touching another rusty nail doesn't make rusting more likely. Zinc or copper nails do not go rusty, though they will tarnish. If iron goes rusty, why do you think is it used? How might rusting be reduced?

Changes in materials

# 4.5 Sweet tea

What do YOU think?

You can investigate what happens by weighing the tea and sugar before and after dissolving. If you don't have a sensitive balance then you can use a lever balance. Level the balance with tea and sugar separately on one side, then dissolve the sugar in the tea and check the balance to see if it has altered. This will show you whether the weight has altered. You could evaporate some sweet tea in a saucer over a radiator to find out whether the sugar is still present in the tea. Does it make a difference if the sugar is put in water not tea?

It's easy to think that when substances dissolve they just vanish. Even though the sugar is not visible when it is dissolved, it is still there. The total weight of the substances when the sugar is dissolved in the tea does not change. The sugar is still there, but not visible. This is why the tea tastes sweet. Do you think sugar will dissolve if you use other liquids? Does it make a difference if you change the temperature of the water? Do you think the answer will be the same for other substances such as salt?

Changes in materials

# 4.6 Acidic oranges

You can't investigate this by tasting things. You don't taste things to see if they are poisonous! Lemons, oranges and other citrus fruits contain citric acid. What other foods contain acids? How will you recognise an acid? You can investigate by using indicators (such as red cabbage juice), or seeing how it reacts with calcium carbonate (in chalk or eggshells). What other tests can you use? Do some acids have more effect than others?

Information in the press about acids suggests that all acids are poisonous and corrosive. This is not correct. Some acids are poisonous and highly corrosive, such as sulphuric acid. Others are not poisonous or highly corrosive, such as citric acid (in citrus fruits) or ethanoic acid (in vinegar). Even when they are very concentrated, these acids are not normally very corrosive or poisonous. What we mean by 'poisonous' is tricky, since virtually everything we eat is damaging if we have too much of it – even essential foods like salt, sugar and water. What else can you find out about which foods are acidic and how they are used in cooking?

# 4.7 Burning candle

You can investigate burning candles by burning a candle wick on its own and burning the wax on its own. Burning the wax is not easy, without using something like a match or a piece of card instead of a wick. Can you tell which bits burn and which do not? Can you collect the gas from a burning candle and find out whether wax condenses from this gas? This will tell you whether the wax has evaporated.

**Safety note:** burning candles must be supervised by an adult.

When a candle is burning, the wick and the wax both burn. The wick only burns very slowly. The wax melts, turns to vapour, and burns. The main reason for having the wick is to draw the molten wax up the wick towards the flame, where it will vaporise and burn. Can you find out whether oil lamps work in the same way as candles?

# 4.8 Melting ice

You can investigate what happens to the weight by weighing an amount of ice before and after it melts, to see whether or not its weight changes. Does the weight change? Does the volume change? Does the density change? Find out about how the density of water alters with changes of temperature. What happens when other liquids freeze? Is it the same as water?

It is easy to get confused about the difference between weight, mass and density. Ice is less dense than water, which is why it floats. When ice melts its mass and its weight do not change. Ten grams of ice will melt to give ten grams of water. However the volume does change when the ice melts. Ten grams of water take up less space than ten grams of ice, so the density of the ice is less than the density of the water. Can you use what you have learnt to explain why icebergs float, where ice forms as water freezes, and how fish manage to survive over the winter when ponds begin to freeze?

# 4.9 Alka Seltzer

It is difficult to do a practical investigation to explore this problem. You can use books or the internet to find out more about what indigestion tablets such as Alka Seltzer are made from. Can you find more examples of reactions where a gas is produced? Can you do any tests to find out what kind of gas is given off? Was this gas present at the start of the reaction? If not, where might it have come from? What kind of reaction is likely to produce a gas? What's the difference between how you get these bubbles and how you get the bubbles in fizzy drinks?

**Safety note:** testing for different gases requires adult supervision.

When the Alka Seltzer tablet and water react they end up in a different physical state. They start as a solid and a liquid, and they change to a liquid and a gas. The gas is produced very rapidly, and this suggests that it is likely to be a chemical reaction, not just a change of state. The bubbles in fizzy drinks are caused by carbon dioxide dissolving in the liquid under pressure. Changes of state are usually easily reversible, but many chemical reactions are not. The reaction between the Alka Seltzer and water isn't easily reversible. This reaction can be used to make Alka Seltzer rockets (you can find instructions for these on the internet). What is the difference between this and the process that propels real rockets into space?

# 4.10 Acid rain

It isn't easy to investigate whether hills dissolve in acid rain. However lots of old buildings are made from the same rocks as the hills. Can you examine old buildings, such as churches, that are made from rock? Are there any signs of damage to the rock? How might the rock get damaged? Is the rock used for building always the same type, or are different rocks used? Can you find out whether samples of rock are damaged by acids? Can you find out whether acid rain has any other effects?

**Safety note:** testing using acids requires adult supervision.

There are lots of different types of rock, and many of these will react with an acid and dissolve. Even very dilute acids can react with some rocks, especially limestone, chalk and marble. More concentrated acids can react with some rocks quickly. Rain is usually acidic. The acidity varies according to factors like industrial pollution and the wind direction. Some hills are reacting with and dissolving in acid rain, but this is usually too slow for us to notice it happening. What do you think are the causes of acid rain?

Changes in materials

# 4.11 Balloons

You can't easily investigate what happens to particles (atoms) as the temperature changes. You can do some research using the internet or books to find evidence to decide which is the most suitable idea. What do you already know about the behaviour of particles in solids, liquids and gases and how this changes with temperature? Perhaps you could do a thought experiment. If particles get bigger at higher temperatures, what would gases be like at very high temperatures (say 1 000 000°C)?

The particles (atoms) that make up air and all substances stay the same size, whatever the temperature. At lower temperatures particles in the air move more slowly (they have less energy). As they move more slowly they get closer together. This means that the volume of gas in the balloon will be less and the balloon will shrink. Although rubber will shrink very slightly at low temperatures, it's the pressure of air inside the balloon that makes the volume of the balloon change. Can you use what you have learnt to explain why hot air balloons rise?

Changes in materials

# 4.12 Rusty nails

You can find out what happens to the weight by weighing the jar of iron nails at the beginning and then after they go rusty. Do you find any change? Does the same thing happen with iron wool? Does it make a difference if the jar has an airtight seal? Does the air inside the jar change when the iron nails go rusty? Do the nails still go rusty if you fill the jar with carbon dioxide? What happens if you use other metals, such as aluminium or stainless steel?

As iron nails go rusty they get heavier. The iron reacts with oxygen in the air to form iron oxide (rust), and the iron oxide is heavier than the iron. This shows that the process taking place is a chemical reaction, not just a physical change. If the jar isn't sealed, then the mass and weight of the jar and nails will become greater as the iron nails react with oxygen in the air. If the jar does have an airtight seal then no more oxygen can get into the jar, so the total mass and weight of the jar and nails will stay the same. Can you explain why stainless steel doesn't rust so easily even though it contains iron?

Changes in materials

# Electricity and magnetism

5

5

# 5.1 Switch

You can arrange a switch in different places in a circuit. What happens to the light when you change the position of the switch? Does the same thing happen with more complicated circuits?

**Safety note:** do not use rechargeable batteries or mains electricity supply in your circuits.

It is easy to think that electricity starts at the battery and goes through each part of the circuit in turn, so that a switch needs to be in front of the lamp to turn it on and off. In fact the electricity flows in all parts of the circuit at the same time. The switch can be anywhere in the circuit and it will still turn the lamp on and off. This doesn't seem obvious, but it's true. What do you think will happen if you use more than one lamp or switch? What kind of materials can you use to make a switch? Are there some that will not work?

# 5.2 Knots

To investigate this problem you need to set up a simple circuit so that the lamp lights up. Now you can tie a knot in the wire. It may be easier to tie a knot in fairly thin wire. What happens when you tie the knot? What happens if you pull the knot tighter or you put the knot in different places?

**Safety note:** do not use rechargeable batteries or mains electricity supply in your circuits.

Electric current is a flow of charged particles (electrons). These are incredibly small, too small to be seen with a microscope. Because they are so small, tying a knot in the wire doesn't normally make any difference to how the electrons move, so the lamp will stay just as bright. Models for electric circuits, such as 'electricity is like water flowing along a hosepipe', can help us to understand more about electric circuits. How well does this model work when thinking about knots in wires?

# 5.3 More wires

To investigate this problem you need to set up a simple circuit so that the lamp lights up. Start with a circuit with single wires connecting the battery to the lamp. What happens to the lamp if you use two wires instead of single wires? What happens if you use three or more wires? Does it matter where in the circuit you put the extra wires?

**Safety note:** do not use rechargeable batteries or mains electricity supply in your circuits.

It is easy to think that if electricity flows down the wire then with more wires there should be more electricity flowing, and the lamp should be brighter. This is not correct. Adding more wires to a circuit does not normally make the lamp shine more brightly. The brightness of the lamp depends on the resistance to the flow of electric current round the circuit, and the number of wires does not normally affect this. What do you think will happen if you use different kinds of wire in the circuit?

# 5.4 Thicker wires

To investigate this problem you need to set up a simple circuit so that the lamp lights up. Start by using normal thickness wires connecting the battery to the lamp. What happens to the lamp if you use thicker wires? What happens if you use thinner wires? Does it matter where in the circuit you put the thicker wires?

**Safety note:** do not use rechargeable batteries or mains electricity supply in your circuits. Very thin wire may get hot.

It is easy to think that if electricity flows down the wire then with thicker wires there should be more electricity flowing and the lamp should be brighter. This is not correct. Using thicker wires in a circuit does not normally make the lamp shine more brightly. The brightness of the lamp depends on the resistance to the flow of electric current round the circuit. The filament in the lamp normally controls the flow of the electric current, not the thickness of wires going to the lamp. However, very thin wires might make the lamp dimmer. Very thin wires in a circuit can get very hot. Can you work out why that might happen?

Electricity and magnetism

# 5.5 Longer wires

To investigate this problem you need to set up a simple circuit so that the lamp lights up. Start with normal length wires connecting the battery to the lamp. What happens to the lamp if you use longer wires? What happens if you use shorter wires? Does it matter where in the circuit you put the longer wires?

**Safety note:** do not use rechargeable batteries or mains electricity supply in your circuits.

It is easy to think that if electricity flows down the wire then with shorter wires there should be more electricity flowing and the lamp should be brighter. This is not correct. Using shorter wires in a circuit does not normally make the lamp shine more brightly. The brightness of the lamp depends on the resistance to the flow of electric current round the circuit. The filament in the lamp normally controls the flow of the electric current, not the length of wires going to the lamp. However, using very long wires might make the lamp dimmer. Do you think that there is any limit to how far electricity can travel along a wire?

# 5.6 Unusual switch

You can investigate this problem by setting up a circuit like the one that is shown. What happens when you complete the circuit? Does anything surprise you? Can you make any other circuits where something surprising happens?

**Safety note:** do not use rechargeable batteries, high voltage batteries or mains electricity supply in this circuit.

In this circuit the switch seems to do the opposite of what it normally does. The switch sets up a low resistance link (usually called a short circuit) between the two terminals of the battery. The thin filament in the lamp has a much higher resistance. The flow of electric current is controlled by the size of the resistance in the circuit. Closing the switch allows the electricity to go through the switch in preference to going through the lamp, so the lamp goes out. This short circuit drains the battery very quickly and gets very hot. Can you think of how this unusual arrangement of switches could be useful?

# 5.7 Circuits

To investigate this problem you need to set up a simple circuit so that the lamp lights up. Now you can change the components. What happens when you use more batteries? What happens when you use bigger batteries? What happens when you use more lamps or bigger lamps? What happens when you use these in different combinations?

**Safety note:** do not use rechargeable batteries or mains electricity supply in your circuits.

Normally with more batteries the voltage will be greater and the lamps will be brighter. With more lamps the resistance will normally be greater and the lamps will be dimmer. However there is no direct relationship between the physical size of a battery and its voltage, and there is no direct relationship between the physical size of a lamp and its resistance. What is the voltage and physical size of the battery inside a watch? What about batteries in other everyday items? Do the smallest lamps used in homes have the lowest voltage?

# 5.8 Street lamps

To investigate this problem you need to set up a simple circuit with lines of lamps wired in different ways. Does the distance from the power supply make any difference to the brightness of the lamps? Does it make any difference if you set up the lamps in series or in parallel? Does anything else make a difference to the brightness?

**Safety note:** do not use rechargeable batteries or mains electricity supply in your circuits.

It is easy to think that electricity starts at the power supply and goes through each lamp in turn, so that lamps nearer the power supply will be brighter than those further away. This is not correct. The electricity flows through each part of the circuit at the same time. All the lamps receive the same amount of electricity. Street lights are wired so that all the lights stay on when one light stops working. If some lights in your circuit were brighter than others, can you work out why that might be?

# 5.9 Christmas tree

To investigate this problem you need to set up a simple circuit with lamps wired in different ways. How can you wire up the lamps? Does it make any difference if you set up the lamps in series or in parallel? Does anything else make a difference to the brightness?

**Safety note:** do not use rechargeable batteries or mains electricity supply in your circuits.

Whether one lamp on its own will be brighter depends on the arrangement of lamps in the circuit. Older Christmas tree lights are often in a series circuit, where each of the lamps is connected in a continuous line. If one lamp breaks, none of them will light. More modern Christmas tree lights are usually in a parallel circuit, where the lamps are connected so that the electricity has alternative routes and can flow through one lamp without having to flow through each of the other lamps. Sometimes these have several parallel circuits working together. If one lamp breaks they don't all go out. Can you find out the differences between LED and incandescent lamps? Is there any difference between them in terms of energy efficiency?

79

# 5.10 Extension lead

To investigate this problem you need to set up a simple circuit. Is an extension lead a complete circuit? Would you expect electricity to flow in the circuit? How will you know if any electricity is leaking out of the end of the wire? Can you use an ammeter to measure the flow of electricity at various points in the circuit? Does this tell you whether any electricity is leaking out?

**Safety note:** do not use rechargeable batteries or mains electricity supply in your circuit.

A complete circuit is needed for electricity to flow. An extension lead can be a part of a complete circuit, but on its own it isn't a complete circuit. The wires in the extension lead end in separate terminals inside the socket, with no direct connection between them. Electricity doesn't leak out of the end of the extension lead. No electricity flows unless something like a toaster is plugged in to the end of the extension lead. If the toaster is switched off, do you think electricity will be flowing through the extension lead? When items such as TVs and computers are left on standby they are said to waste energy. Do you think this is because the electricity leaks out? How much energy is wasted?

Electricity and magnetism

# 5.11 Current flow

To investigate this problem you need to set up a simple circuit. Now you can find out how much electric current there is in each wire by using an ammeter to measure the electric current at different points round the circuit. What do you notice? Is there more electric current in one of the wires? Does anything seem to be lost going round the circuit? Does using an analogy, like water flow in central heating systems, help to make sense of what is happening?

**Safety note:** do not use rechargeable batteries or mains electricity supply in your circuit.

It is easy to think that there will be more electric current going to the lamp than going away from it. This is not correct. The current is the same all the way round the circuit. Since the batteries go flat, something must be being 'used up' in the circuit, but it isn't the electric current. The electric current is a bit like the water in a central heating system, carrying energy round to the radiators but without being used up. The electric current is made up of electrons that carry energy round the circuit. The energy can be transferred at the lamp, but the electric current stays the same all the way round the circuit. How do you think rechargeable batteries work? Do they get refilled with current?

# 5.12 Electromagnet

To investigate this problem you need to set up a circuit like the one shown. Now you can try each of the alternatives. Does it make any difference if you use a nail? Does it make any difference if you use insulated or non-insulated wire? How will you measure how good the electromagnet is? Could you use a compass needle, or get the electromagnet to attract objects such as paperclips?

**Safety note:** do not use rechargeable batteries or mains electricity supply in your circuit.

When electric current flows along a wire it generates a magnetic effect. The magnetic effect is most obvious when the wire is wound into a coil. The magnetic effect is stronger if you wind the wire round a nail or another soft iron object, but the magnetic effect will still be produced with just the wire. You can use non-insulated wire, but the electromagnet works better with insulated wire so that the electric current flows along the wire and not directly into the nail. What happens to the electromagnet as you increase the number of loops in the coil?

# Forces and motion

6

# 6.1 Bungee jumpers

To investigate this problem you need to drop different objects to see what happens. What might make a difference? You could explore things such as weight, surface area and shape. Remember to choose one thing to investigate, and then keep the other things the same in your investigation. Which of these might make a difference?

It is easy to think that heavy things fall faster than light things. The force of gravity is greater on a heavier object, but a heavier object also needs more force to make it move. So the two people will fall at about the same rate. Air resistance can make a difference to how an object falls, especially if it has a large surface area. In this situation it shouldn't make much difference. The bigger, heavier person will pull more (exert a bigger force) on the elastic at the bottom of the fall, so the elastic will stretch more. What do you think will happen if you use different thicknesses of elastic?

# 6.2 Falling

What can you do to the paper to make it fall faster? Does screwing it up, or folding it into a dart shape, make a difference? What happens if you change the shape of the feather, or drop it in different ways? What happens if you combine things, like a piece of paper and a paper clip? See if you can find video footage of the first lunar astronauts dropping a hammer and a feather on the Moon. How do things fall on the Moon? What can you learn from this?

If you screw up the paper, or cut the vanes off the feather, it will fall faster. This suggests that the feather and paper fall slowly because of their large surface area. Things with a large surface area catch the air, creating a lot of air resistance, and this slows down the rate of falling. Things that have a small surface area, like a paper clip, usually fall quickly. How does this help you to understand how parachutes work?

Forces and motion

# 6.3 Magnets

You can find out which is the strongest magnet by carrying out simple practical tests. For example, how many pins or paper clips will a magnet pick up? Will a magnet pick up a nail? What other simple tests could you do? Are some magnets stronger than others? Are some parts of a magnet stronger than others?

The shape and size of a magnet don't make much difference to the amount of magnetic force. The amount of magnetic force depends on what material the magnet is made from, how strongly it is magnetised and how the particles are arranged inside the magnet. You can't tell which magnet is the strongest without testing them. What are very strong magnets used for?

# 6.4 Hot air balloon

You don't need to use a hot air balloon to test this. Can you weigh some people before and after they eat, then find out whether the weight of people plus food has changed? What if you have people and food balanced on one end of a seesaw? Will the seesaw change if the people eat the food? Is the amount of food the same, whether it is outside or inside the body? What else might affect the weight of the hot air balloon?

If the passengers eat the food, it won't make any difference to the weight (or mass) of the balloon and passengers. Over a longer period of time the food is metabolised by the body. Most of it ends up as carbon dioxide and water. These are breathed out from the lungs, so the balloon and passengers will slowly get lighter! What do you think would happen if they were inside a sealed space, like a space rocket?

# 6.5 Ski slope

How many things can you think of that might make a difference to the way things slide down slopes? You can find out by sliding objects down a ramp and measuring how fast they slide. What seems to make a difference? You could use a piece of curtain rail as a track and roll marbles down it. You could make blocks of ice and slide them down a slope, and this will give you a good idea of what happens when you slide on snow or ice. How can you speed them up and slow them down?

When you slide down a hill, you accelerate because of gravity. It's like falling. The force of gravity is greater on a heavier object, but a heavier object also needs more force to make it move. So like bungee jumpers falling through the air, heavy or light skiers should come down at about the same speed. Air resistance is a more important factor. The effect of the skis is quite complicated. The size of skis makes more difference to control than to speed of sliding. How does using knowledge about sliding help skiers to go faster?

# 6.6 Skateboard

You can find out more about forces by using objects that roll or slide, and pushing them to see how far they go. What happens if you push them with different amounts of force? What happens when you slide them on different surfaces – a polished floor, a carpet, gravel or grass? Try sliding a piece of ice on a polished surface. What do you notice about how quickly things slow down and how much they keep moving?

It is easy to think that objects need a force to keep them moving. This is not correct. Moving objects slow down because friction slows them down. If there is no friction and no other force acting, then the object will keep on moving in the same direction and at the same speed. We take friction for granted and don't really notice when it is acting. The skateboard slows down because of friction. There is no force to keep the skateboard moving, except when she pushes herself along with her foot. Can you think of situations where friction is helpful or unhelpful?

Forces and motion

# 6.7 Football

> **If I kick the ball hard enough it will never came down**

> **It comes down because it runs out of force**

> **It comes down because there is no upwards force after you have kicked it**

> **It comes down because gravity pulls it down**

## What do YOU think?

It isn't easy to measure the forces on the football, so doing a practical investigation is difficult. You could do a book or an internet search to find out more about forces. Can you do a thought experiment to predict what would happen if the ball needs a force to keep moving? How would a paper aeroplane or a javelin keep on flying after someone has thrown it? How would a space rocket travel to the Moon? Can you work out what would happen if an astronaut on the Moon kicks a football?

It is easy to think that moving objects must have a force pushing them in the direction that they are moving. This is not correct. After you kick it there is no upwards force on the football. When the football is in the air, the only forces are gravity pulling it down towards the Earth, and a small force due to air resistance. If you could kick it hard enough, in theory it would never come down (like satellites that can stay permanently above the Earth), but in practice this is not possible. How are the forces on a football different from the forces on an aeroplane?

# 6.8 Space rocket

**What do YOU think?**

Speech bubbles:
- I think the rocket will slow down gradually
- The rocket will just float in space now that it has run out of fuel
- I think the rocket will fall towards the nearest planet
- I think the rocket will carry on moving at the same speed

You can't do a practical investigation to find out what will happen to the rocket. You can do a book or an internet search to find out more. Can you do a thought experiment to predict what would happen in space? Would the gravity from a planet be strong enough to attract the rocket? Is there any friction in space to slow down the rocket? How do the Earth and the other planets travel in their orbits round the Sun?

On Earth friction slows down moving objects. In space there is virtually no atmosphere and therefore virtually no friction. If the space rocket is some distance away from the Earth's gravitational field, then it will keep moving at the same speed and in the same direction after its fuel runs out. If it gets close enough to another star or planet, then it will be affected by their gravitational field and gradually fall towards the star or planet. Science fiction films show space rockets switching on their gravity shields. Do you think this is possible?

Forces and motion

# 6.9 Elephant feet

Don't try this! You should be able to predict what will happen. How much does a typical elephant weigh? How big are its feet? What is the pressure under each foot? What does that feel like? You can set up a model, using blocks of wood and modelling clay, to check your prediction. You should be able to use reference sources, such as books or the internet, to check your answer. Would it make a difference if the elephant was walking or running?

Elephants are big and heavy. The bottom of the elephant's foot has a large surface area. Whether your foot gets damaged depends on the pressure underneath the elephant's foot. The pressure will depend on the area of the elephant's foot, its weight, how many feet are on the ground and how much of its feet are in contact with the ground. We think that it would be painful but probably would not completely crush your foot. We haven't tried this! Would it be more painful for an elephant or someone wearing stiletto heels to stand on your foot?

# 6.10 Fast plane

You can find out more about acceleration, speed and journey time by doing some simple calculations. What about some extreme examples, such as a person accelerates quickly to 6 kilometres per hour, and a car accelerates slowly to 100 kilometres per hour? Which will cover 1000 km faster? You could draw distance-time graphs or use computer simulations. If you use runners or bicycles in a playground to model this situation, what does this tell you about how acceleration, speed and journey time are connected?

Journey time depends on average speed, not acceleration. Rapid acceleration helps to get the plane up to its top speed quickly. Over short distances acceleration will make a difference to the journey time. Over long distances maximum speed is much more important than acceleration. Having good acceleration does not mean that the top speed must be greater. What can you find out about the acceleration and top speed of a range of animals? How does this help them to survive?

Forces and motion

# 6.11 Space walk

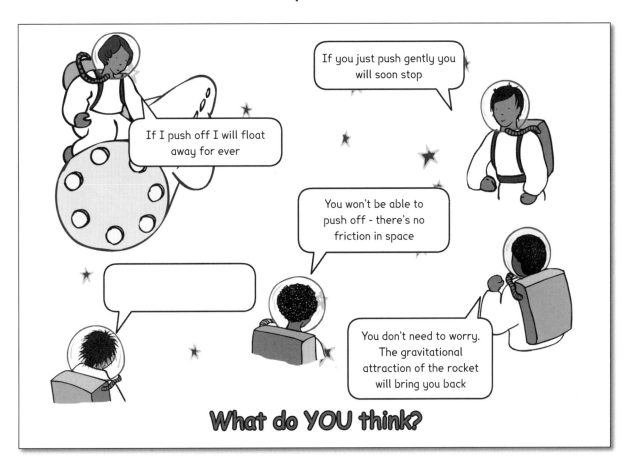

You can't do a practical investigation to find out what will happen in space. You can think about what forces might make the astronaut slow down. Is there any air resistance, friction or gravity in space? There are video clips on the NASA website that show what happens to astronauts and objects in space. Can you find out what real astronauts do if they have to go outside their space rocket to fix a problem?

Astronauts who go on a space walk need a good understanding of how forces operate! If the astronaut pushes off in any direction then s/he will just float away, since there are virtually no forces to prevent movement. The astronaut has to be to be attached to the space rocket. The astronaut will be attracted by the gravitational attraction of the rocket, but this force is much too small to prevent someone from floating away. Why do you think astronauts float around inside their space vehicle?

# 6.12 Moon rock

You can't do a practical investigation to find out what will happen with rocks in a tank of water on the Moon. Start with finding out about floating and sinking on Earth. Why do things float or sink? What difference does density make? Do things float differently in different liquids? This should help you to make predictions about what might happen on the Moon. Do all rocks sink in water on Earth?

Gravity is much less on the Moon than it is on Earth, so the rock weighs less on the Moon than on Earth. The mass and volume of the rock have not changed, so its density has not changed. The same is true of the water – it weighs less but its density has not changed. Therefore the relationship between the density of the rock and the density of the water has not changed. So the rock will sink on the Moon. However the force of gravity on the Moon is smaller than it is on Earth, so the rock will sink more slowly. What do you think would happen if you took the tank of water and rocks into space on a rocket?

# Light

7

Light

# 7.1 Seeing in the dark

You need to find a dark room or create a dark area to test the different possibilities. A room with no windows is ideal. You can drape thick black cloth over a table, or even use a very large cardboard box to create a dark area. Take different objects into the dark area. What will you choose? What can you see? Can you see the different objects in complete darkness? How much light do you need before you can see things?

It is easy to think that it is possible to see in the dark because most people have not been in complete darkness. Our eyes adjust so that we can see in different levels of light, but they can't adjust to seeing when there is no light at all. In complete darkness we can't see anything. If we use a light source like a torch then we can see objects as the light from the torch bounces off them. Where will it be completely dark? How do you think owls see at night?

# 7.2 Shadow screen

You can find out about shadows by setting up a screen with a bright light shining on it. You can make a shadow by standing between the lamp and screen, or you can use cardboard cut-out figures. Try moving the objects. How do the shadows change? What do you think is happening to the light? How do you think a shadow is formed? Can you draw a simple diagram to show what happens?

If the person is closer to the light source, then more of the light will be blocked. So the shadow will be biggest when the person stands close to the lamp. This is because the rays of light from the lamp spread out in all directions, so close to the lamp the person will block more of the light rays. If you use the Sun as a light source then the rays of light will be parallel, and the distance from the screen makes no difference to the size of the shadow. Can you find any other differences between the shadows when you stand in front of a lamp and shadows from the Sun?

# 7.3 Curved mirror

Find some curved mirrors, such as make-up mirrors or car wing mirrors. Have a look at the image in the mirror. Does it make any difference how far away the mirror is? Does it make any difference if the mirror is more or less curved? Are the images the right way up? Are the images the right way round? What size are the images? How do the images in a convex mirror compare with the images in a concave mirror?

With a convex mirror the image is always the right way up. With a concave mirror the image can be the right way up or upside down, depending on how curved the mirror is and how far away the object is. What matters is the position of the object in relation to the focal point (the point at which parallel rays of light that are reflected from the mirror usually cross). If the object is closer than the focal point then the image will be the right way up and bigger. If the object is further away then the image will be upside down and either bigger or smaller, depending on the distance. Can mirrors change images in any other ways? How does the way mirrors change images help in everyday life?

# 7.4 White cat

You need to find a dark room or create a dark area to test the different possibilities. A room with no windows is ideal. You can drape thick black cloth over a table, or even use a very large cardboard box to create a dark area. Make sure that no light is getting in. Then you can take different objects into the dark area. Try shiny objects, such as coins or aluminium foil, and white objects, such as a white shirt or piece of paper. What can you see? Can you see the different objects in complete darkness? How do you think 'cat's eyes' in a road work?

It is easy to think that a cat's eyes glow in the dark and that we can see white objects in the dark, but this is not correct. We rarely experience complete darkness, so what we call 'dark' isn't completely dark. Most of the time there is some light around at night. The cat's eyes and white fur both reflect light. When some light is present they reflect it and we can see them clearly. In complete darkness there is no light to be reflected, so we won't see the white cat or its eyes. Are there any things that we can see in complete darkness? How can you use what you have learnt to explain why it's a good idea to wear light clothes when riding a bike at night? The Moon doesn't have any light of its own, so how can we see it on a dark night?

# 7.5 Green shadows

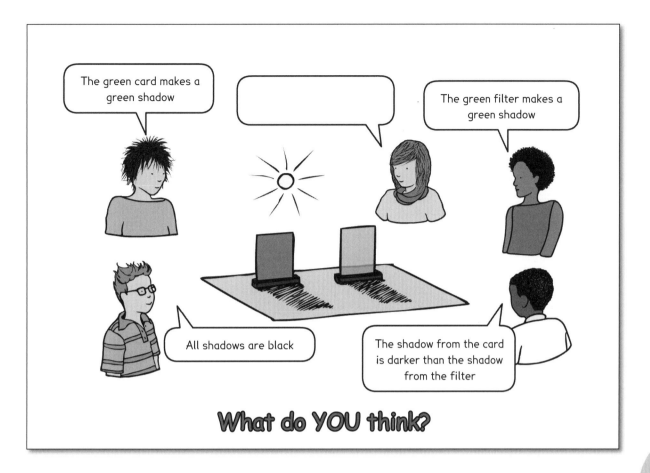

You can find out about shadows using a lamp and different objects to make the shadows. Put the objects on a white surface to make the shadows more visible. You can compare the shadows made by pale or dark-coloured objects, dull or reflective surfaces, opaque or transparent materials, and white or coloured light sources. What do you notice? Are all the shadows the same? Can you find out what materials are used to make shadow puppets?

A shadow is the absence of light, so in most situations shadows are black. With a coloured filter, some of the light is absorbed but some colours of light pass through. So the shadow will be an area of reduced light that is coloured. A green filter lets green light pass through to produce a green shadow. The green card lets no light through, so the shadow will be black. Since the card blocks all of the light the shadow from the card will be darker than the shadow from the filter. If very glossy card is used then there may be some reflection from the surface of the card, so the shadow may have a faint green tinge. In what circumstances can shadows look coloured?

# 7.6 Moving shadow

You can set up a stick so that it makes a shadow, then watch how the shadow moves and measure the movement of the shadow during the daytime. See how long it takes for the shadow to move a certain amount. You could measure this as a distance or as degrees around a circle. Set up a globe and light source, with a cocktail stick to make a shadow, and see how the shadow moves as you turn the globe. This should help you to understand how the shadow forms and why it moves. Do you think you will get the same pattern with shadows formed by moonlight?

The Earth rotates on its axis once every 24 hours, so it will take 24 hours, not 12 hours, for the shadow of the stick to return to its original position. This means that the shadow moves through $360°$ in 24 hours, which is approximately $15°$ per hour. Depending on where you are on the Earth's surface the movement of the shadow may not be exactly $15°$ per hour. Did you find that in your measurements? What will be the difference in the way that the shadow moves round the stick in the Northern and Southern Hemispheres? What about at the equator?

# 7.7 Sunglasses

You can find out about the amount of light if you have access to a light meter or data logging equipment. Wait for a snowy day, then measure the amount of sunlight landing on the snow and compare this with the amount of light reflected from the snow. How does the amount of light compare? If it doesn't snow then you could use artificial snow or ground up ice as a substitute. If snow stores or generates light you should be able to see it in a dark room and measure how much light is released from the snow. What do you think will happen?

Sunlight reflects well off white or shiny surfaces. Snow is white, so sunlight reflects off the snow very well. The snow doesn't produce or store any light. It simply reflects light from the Sun. The reflection from the snow increases the total amount of sunlight shining on you. Bright moonlight on snow can look almost as bright as daylight. Why do people who go skiing, or who live in snowy places, need sunglasses and sun cream in winter?

You can find out about the shadows that trees make if you can find some trees growing close together. You could make a model, using trees cut out of card to make some shadows. What do you notice where the shadows overlap? What happens if you use translucent objects to make overlapping shadows? Are the trees opaque, translucent or transparent? Do transparent objects make shadows?

A shadow is an area of reduced light. If two shadows overlap then the two shadows don't usually add together to make an even darker shadow. The way that the leaves on a tree are arranged means that there can be gaps where some light might get through. This makes it complicated to predict what exactly will happen. If there are two trees there might be fewer patches of light on the ground. If some light passes through the leaves the shadow could be a bit darker where the two shadows overlap. What happens if coloured shadows overlap?

# 7.9 Torches

It isn't easy to measure how far light travels. You could use a book or search the internet to help you. Why not try a thought experiment and predict what should happen? What about how brightly different torches shine? You should be able to measure this with a light meter or data logger. What about the area that they light up? You should be able to measure this too, by shining the torches onto a piece of black paper. Why do we see some stars in the sky more clearly than others?

Light normally travels at the same speed, whatever light source produces it. There is no limit to the distance it will travel. However the brightness of the light and the area lit up can be different. A brighter torch can illuminate an area more brightly, illuminate a bigger area, or both. The brightness doesn't depend on the size of the torch – you can have a large dim torch or a small bright torch. What will happen to the light if you shine a torch up into the sky at night?

# 7.10 Mirror box

You can find out about what will happen with a mirror box by making a box completely lined with mirrors. Shine a light into the box, shut the lid and then open it in a completely dark area. Do you see any light come out of the box? You can use a data logger, with a light sensor inside the box, to record the light levels before and after the lid is shut. This should help you to decide what happens to the light inside the box. Can you find out how mirrors are used to capture solar energy?

Light is a type of radiation, not a tangible substance. Most of the light is reflected by the mirrors, but some of the light is not reflected and is absorbed by the mirrors. As the light bounces around inside the box, all of the light is absorbed. As the light is absorbed the energy has to end up somewhere, so the temperature of the box will increase by a tiny amount, though not enough to measure. Is it possible to shut the lid of the box fast enough to trap any light inside?

# 7.11 Prism

You can find out about light by investigating coloured lights, filters and paints, and combining them in different ways. What colours do you get from different combinations of lights? What colours do you get from different combinations of filters? What colours do you get from different combinations of paints? Can you use more than one prism to separate and then recombine the colours in white light?

A prism can split white light into different colours. With two or more prisms it is possible to recombine the different colours to make white light. Different coloured lights can be mixed to produce white light. Coloured filters or paints look coloured because they absorb some of the colours from white light. Adding more paint or more filters in front of a light source will absorb more and more colours from white light, so eventually the result is grey or black, not white. If plants need light to grow, which colours of light do they need if they normally have green leaves?

You can't do a simple practical investigation to find out what happens to the stars. Can you set up a model to show what happens to the stars during the day? Can you find a CD or an internet site where someone has produced an animated model of what happens? Can you visit an interactive science centre where there are models or animations? Can you find the North Star in the Northern Hemisphere, or the Southern Cross in the Southern Hemisphere, during the night and predict where it will be during the day?

Unlike the Moon, stars generate their own light. They are still there even during the daytime, so why can't we see them? The stars are huge distances away from the Earth, so very little light from them reaches the Earth. The Sun is the only star that is close to the Earth. The Sun is so much brighter compared to the other stars that we can't see the faint light from the other stars during the daytime. Can you find out which is the brightest star in our night sky? How far away is it? If we can't see the stars during the day, why can we sometimes see the Moon during the day?

# Sound

8

# 8.1 Drums

You can find out more about the sound a drum makes if you have drums of different shapes and sizes. Hit each drum and listen carefully to the sound it makes. Real drums will be best, but you can make drums of different sizes by stretching something like cling film tightly over a hollow container. What happens to the surface of the drum when you hit it? Putting grains of rice on the surface might help you to see what is happening.

Several things make a difference to the sound produced by a hollow object. The shape, the size and the way you hit the drum all make a difference. The skin of the drum vibrates to make the sound. The more you stretch the skin on a drum, the higher the pitch of the sound it makes. Normally bigger drums make a lower-pitched sound that lasts for longer (resonates), but it might not always make a louder sound. The loudness of the drum will depend on how hard you hit it. How does the material that the drum is made from affect the sound and loudness?

# 8.2 Pipes

You can find out more about how sound is carried by comparing how well pipes full of air or water carry sounds. Does it make a difference if the pipes are made of metal or plastic? How will you decide how well the sound is carried? Think about how data logging equipment could help. How well would the sound be carried through a solid piece of metal?

Sounds can travel through lots of different materials, including air, water and metal, so all of these could carry sound in a radiator pipe. The vibrations that we hear as sound need something to carry them. Generally solids carry sound vibrations better than liquids, and liquids carry them better than gases. So the metal pipes should carry the sound better than the water or air in the pipes. Sometimes noises through pipes can be a nuisance. How could these noises be reduced?

# 8.3 Ear trumpet

You can make a simple ear trumpet from a rolled up piece of card or paper. How do sounds compare with or without the ear trumpet? Can you tell what direction the sounds come from? Using a blindfold will help you to investigate the ear trumpet accurately. Will it make a difference if the ear trumpet is short and fat or long and thin? What if it is a large flat flap, like an elephant's ear, rather than a trumpet?

The ear trumpet acts like a funnel that collects sound. It can collect more sound waves because it has a large open end. This means that the sound will be louder. The direction that the ear trumpet faces makes a difference to the sound that you hear, so you will hear sounds better from one side than the other. How do a rabbit's ears help it to avoid being caught by predators?

# 8.4 Mirror

**What do YOU think?**

You can use different types of surfaces to find out how well they reflect sounds. You can shout at the different surfaces, but it is better to use a standard sound, like a ticking clock. Using a sound sensor and data logger to measure the sound will make the investigation more accurate. How will you prevent the sensor picking up the sound of the clock as well as the reflected sound? Does using different sound sources make a difference to what happens?

Mirrors are good at reflecting sound as well as light. Hard, smooth, polished surfaces are usually good sound reflectors, while soft, rough or fluffy surfaces act as sound absorbers or insulators. Polished surfaces reflect light in one direction instead of scattering it in all directions, and the same effect happens with sound waves. A curved mirror will concentrate the sound waves, just like it concentrates light rays. Some telescopes work by detecting radio waves. Can you use what you have learnt to work out how this kind of telescope might work?

# 8.5 Noisy bus

You can find out how well sounds are reflected or absorbed by comparing the sounds in rooms with or without curtains, with or without carpets, and so on. If you have a data logger and a sound sensor then you could make a model by lining a large cardboard box or a cupboard with different materials, and comparing how well sounds are reflected or absorbed. Which material is best at absorbing sounds?

Hard, smooth and polished surfaces reflect sound well. Buses that have a lot of these surfaces are noisy. Unfurnished rooms can also be noisy because of the number of hard surfaces, like walls and floorboards. Using more soft, rough or fluffy surfaces, such as curtains, carpets and fabric seats, helps to absorb the sounds and make the room quieter. How can you use what you have learnt to design different kinds of living spaces? What can you find out about noise pollution in the environment and how it can be controlled?

# 8.6 Swimming pool

It isn't easy to measure sounds in a swimming pool. You could set up a model to find out how well sound is reflected from different surfaces, including water. A sound sensor and data logging equipment will help you to do this. Then you can predict the effect of these surfaces at a swimming pool. Do sounds change in any other ways at a swimming pool?

An indoor swimming pool is usually noisy when people are swimming. Hard, smooth, tiled surfaces reflect sounds well, and the water surface also reflects a lot of sound. Sounds made by the swimmers will be reflected rather than absorbed. This means that you hear echoes. The surfaces only reflect the sound, they don't create sound. Any materials used at the swimming pool will need to be waterproof, so it isn't easy to reduce the sound levels by using softer materials, like curtains and carpets. Can you find out more about how sound reflection is managed in concert halls?

# 8.7 Aeroplane

What do YOU think?

It isn't easy to investigate where the sound comes from unless you live near an airport or on a flight path. Can you work out what will happen with the aeroplane by finding out more about thunder and lightning? Do you hear the thunder or see the lightning first? Why is this? Can you do something similar over shorter distances, such as across a field, by bashing cymbals together and finding out whether someone can see them or hear them first? Does the type of sound make a difference to how long it takes for the sound to arrive?

Light travels much faster than sound, so the aeroplane can usually be seen before it is heard. By the time the sound of the plane reaches you, the plane will have travelled partway across the sky (unless the plane is very close). If the plane is some distance away, you will need to look in front of where the sound seems to come from to see the plane. Can you use what you have learnt to find out how a sonic boom happens? Do an internet search for pictures of sonic booms.

# 8.8 Stethoscope

You can find out about what happens with a stethoscope by exploring how sound travels through a wide range of materials. Find a way to make some sounds inside a cardboard box – for example, using a ticking clock. Then try using different objects and materials (e.g. a wooden stick, string, a metal bar, a plastic tube), to listen to the sounds inside the box. Use some that are not straight (e.g. a coiled spring). When can you hear the sound inside the box? Which materials are best at carrying the sound

Sounds are carried through solids, liquids and gases, and they can go round bends and through obstructions. A stethoscope is a hollow rubber tube filled with air. Most of the sound in the stethoscope is carried by the air, so a knot will stop most of the sound travelling. Some of the sound can be carried by the rubber tube, so the knot may not stop all of the sound. If sound travels through lots of different materials, why do earplugs make sounds quieter?

# 8.9 Windy day

What do YOU think?

This isn't easy to investigate. If you have a sound sensor and data logging equipment then you can set up a model inside a room, with a sound that you can measure. Use a fan to blow an air current between the sound source and the sound sensor. Does it make any difference to the sound? Does it make any difference if the wind is blowing towards or away from you?

Sounds waves travel through the air. If the air is moving then sound waves will travel faster in the direction that the air is moving. Even when it is windy, the sound can travel through the air so you will still hear the sound. If the wind blows towards you then you will hear sounds better than if it blows away from you. What happens if the wind blows sideways through the space between the sound and the receiver?

# 8.10 Moon walk

Although you aren't able to go to the Moon, the important point about hearing on the Moon is that there is no air. You can find out what happens to sounds if there is no air. Do a search on the internet for sounds inside a bell jar. You can find out what happens to a sound inside a jar if the air is taken out of the jar. Does this help you to work out what will happen on the Moon? Where will the sound go to if an astronaut shouts inside the helmet?

Visible light and radio waves can travel through a vacuum, but sound needs something to carry it. Since there is no air on the Moon there is nothing to carry the sound. The astronauts wouldn't hear any sounds if they were able to take their helmets off. If they put their helmets together so the helmets are touching, then they should be able to hear some sound through the helmets. Some people use a drinking glass against a wall to hear what people are saying on the other side of the wall. How do you think this might work?

# 8.11 Radio

You can find out what happens to sound underwater by wrapping a battery-powered or wind-up radio in a polythene bag to keep out the water. Can you hear the sound if the radio is underwater? Can you hear the sound better if you put one ear under the water? The easiest way to investigate this is in a bath or at a swimming pool. Can you hear people talking at the side of the swimming pool if you swim underwater?

**Safety note:** do not use a plug-in radio.

Sound waves travel well in both air and water. You should be able to hear a waterproof radio playing if you take it underwater with you. How sound travels where it passes from air to water or water to air is more complicated. Sound doesn't usually travel well across an air/water boundary. If the radio is on the beach you won't hear it underwater, and if it is underwater you won't hear it on the beach. Can you use what you have learnt to explain how animals that live in the sea communicate with each other and when it might be possible for humans to hear them? Can you find out how far sounds will carry in water?

# 8.12 Guitarist

This one is different. People often expect Concept Cartoons to be humorous, and they are surprised when they can't see the joke. So here is an example of a Concept Cartoon that we have included simply to make you smile. But you might use it to start a very interesting discussion. Over to you!

# Earth and beyond

9

6

Earth and beyond

# 9.1 24 Hours

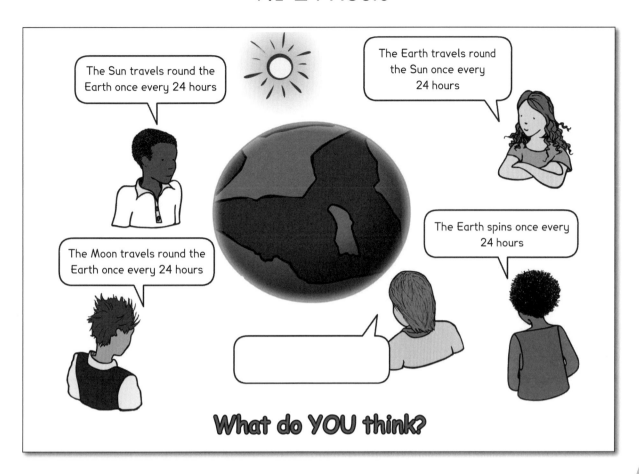

You can't do a simple practical investigation to solve this problem. Try setting up some sort of model, with a globe and strong light source, to work out what is happening. You could try a thought experiment to predict what would happen for each alternative. Simulations on videos or CDs should help you. What about a visit to a science centre to see a demonstration? If it is daytime where you live on the Earth, will it be night-time anywhere else at the same time?

Day and night are caused by the Earth rotating on its axis. As it rotates, the position of the Sun in the sky appears to change. The rotation happens every 24 hours, so we get the familiar 24-hour cycle of light and dark. Although it looks like the Sun is travelling across the sky, this is because we don't notice that the Earth is rotating. We think that the Sun really is moving, rather than the Earth moving. How can you show that the Earth orbits around the Sun?

# 9.2 Summer Sun

How will you find out about the position of the Sun? Try recording where it is in the sky at different times of year. An internet or book search may help you to find out where it is in the sky in different countries. Does the temperature change in the summer appear to be related to the height of the Sun in the sky? What happens to the temperature inside the Arctic Circle, where the Sun is visible in the sky all day in the middle of summer?

**Safety note:** don't look directly at the Sun.

The Sun appears to move across the sky each day. It is higher in the sky during the summer and is visible for longer. When the Sun is higher in the sky, its rays are spread over a smaller area of the Earth's surface, and the more concentrated rays make the temperature higher. Hot countries are generally those where the Sun is highest, though other factors also affect temperature. Why isn't it hot on Mount Everest when the Sun is high in the sky?

Earth and beyond

# 9.3 Moonlight

Try observing the Moon very closely when it is a half or quarter Moon, using a telescope or pair of binoculars. Look at the part that is in darkness as well as the part that is bright. What can you see? Does this tell you whether or not the Moon creates its own light? What can you find out about lunar eclipses? What does this tell you about whether the Moon reflects light from the Earth or from the Sun?

It is easy to think that the Moon is a source of light, like the Sun. This is not correct. The Sun generates light itself while the Moon just reflects light from the Sun. If the Moon did generate its own light then all of its surface would be bright, not just part of the surface. Do you think that the Earth can reflect light?

# 9.4 Daytime Moon

You can find out what happens to the Moon by observing its position in the sky every 24 hours and recording this for a month. Does the Moon's movement follow a regular pattern? Can you start to predict where the Moon will be and what it will look like? You can search the internet for models or video clips of how the Moon changes. Can you work out what is happening when the Moon isn't visible in the sky

The Moon comes up and goes down in the sky, but this does not follow the same 24-hour pattern as the Sun. The Moon does not rise at the same time each day and its position in the sky changes daily. It takes slightly more than 29 days to return to the same position in the sky. Sometimes the Moon can be seen during the daytime, with the Sun and Moon visible at the same time. Why doesn't the Moon appear next to the Sun during the day?

# 9.5 Eclipse

You can't do a simple practical investigation to solve this problem. You can set up some sort of model, with a globe and strong light source and a small ball to represent the Moon, to work out what is happening. You can do a thought experiment to predict what would happen for each alternative. Have a look at simulations on videos or CDs. You could visit a science centre and see a demonstration. The Sun and the Moon look about the same size in the sky, so does this mean that they are about the same distance from the Earth?

We get an eclipse of the Sun when the Moon passes between the Earth and the Sun, so the Moon blocks out the Sun's light and the Earth is in the Moon's shadow. This does not happen very often because they need to line up exactly. It can only happen with the Moon since no other planetary body is close enough to the Earth to block out the Sun's light. Can you work out how an eclipse of the Moon might happen?

# 9.6 Winter Sun

You can't do a simple practical investigation to solve this problem. You can set up some sort of model, with a globe and strong light source, to work out what is happening. You can do a thought experiment to predict what would happen for each alternative. Have a look at simulations on videos or CDs. You can visit a science centre and see a demonstration. What happens in winter in other countries? You can make links with schools elsewhere through Science Across the World on the ASE website (www.ase.org.uk).

The winter Sun doesn't shine as strongly or for as long during the day as the summer Sun. This is because light from the Sun strikes the Earth at a different angle during the winter compared to the summer. During summer in the Northern Hemisphere this part of the Earth is angled more towards the Sun, so sunlight strikes this part of the Earth more directly and it gets warmer. The opposite happens in winter. The Sun hasn't changed and it isn't further away. What happens to the Sun in the winter at the North Pole?

Earth and beyond

# 9.7 Moon shape

You can't do a simple practical investigation to solve this problem. You can set up some sort of model, with a globe and strong light source and a small ball to represent the Moon, to work out what is happening. You can do a thought experiment to predict what would happen for each alternative. Simulations on videos or CDs should help you, and so can a visit to a science centre or watching a demonstration. Can you work out how an eclipse of the Moon might happen?

We only see the part of the Moon that is lit by the Sun. As the Moon, Earth and Sun change their positions, we look at the Moon from a different angle, so the Moon seems to change shape. When the Earth does make a shadow on the Moon it causes an eclipse of the Moon. Why don't we get a lunar eclipse every month?

Earth and beyond

# 9.8 Rotating Earth

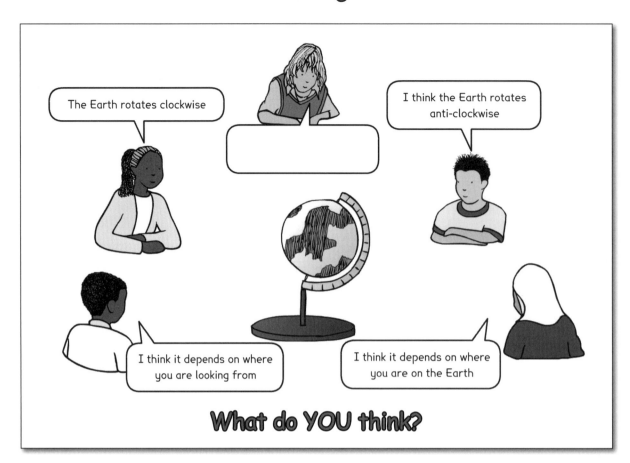

You can find out about which way the Earth turns by setting up a model. Use a globe with bits of modelling clay stuck on at different points to represent people. Stick these at the North Pole and the South Pole. What will each of them see when they look down at their feet? Which way will the Earth appear to turn? Which way will shadows move on a sundial?

To someone in the Northern Hemisphere the Earth appears to rotate anti-clockwise. But to someone in the Southern Hemisphere the Earth appears to rotate clockwise. Which way it seems to rotate depends on where you are looking from. There are no absolute directions in space, so the only way to describe the rotation of the Earth is in relation to a particular point on Earth. Which way will the Earth appear to rotate to someone at the equator?

Earth and beyond

# 9.9 Outer space

You can't do a simple practical investigation to solve this problem. You can set up some sort of model, with a globe and strong light source, to work out what is happening. You could try a thought experiment to predict whether it will be light or dark in space. It could be interesting to contact an astronomer to find out what he or she thinks about it. How dark will it be in the shadow of a planet?

Comics and films promote the idea that outer space is completely dark, but this may not always be true. Objects will be brightly lit if they are reasonably near to the Sun, or near to any other star. If they are further away they will not be brightly lit. Empty space will be very dark, but even here there will be some dim light from distant stars. Will an astronaut in a space rocket see day and night?

# 9.10 Dark Side of the Moon

You can't do a simple practical investigation to solve this problem. You can set up some sort of model, with a globe and strong light source and a small ball to represent the Moon, to work out what is happening. What do you see if you look at the Moon with binoculars? Simulations on videos or CDs should help you. A visit to a science centre and seeing a demonstration should give you some useful ideas. Will the Moon have day and night like we do on Earth?

Although we talk about the dark side of the Moon, in reality it doesn't have a dark side. The Moon rotates once for each orbit around the Earth. This means that it always faces the same way in relation to the Earth. It has a face that we never see from Earth. Although we call this the dark side, for about half of the time it is brightly lit by the Sun. We call it the dark side because we never see it. Will the Moon have two dark sides in a lunar eclipse?

# 9.11 Movement of the Sun

You can find out about which way the Sun moves by setting up a model. Use a globe with bits of modelling clay stuck on at different points to represent people. Stick these in the Northern Hemisphere and the Southern Hemisphere. What will each of them see as the Sun rises and sets? Can you predict what will happen to the Sun and to shadows on the ground? Get evidence from photographs or videos to see if your predictions are correct. Will sundials be different in the Northern and Southern Hemispheres?

The direction of movement is the same all the way through the year. To an observer in most of the Northern Hemisphere, the Sun appears to rise in the east, go round to the south and set in the west. To an observer in most of the Southern Hemisphere, the Sun appears to rise in the east, go round to the north and set in the west. Near the equator the movement appears more complicated. What will a person at the equator see?

# 9.12 Moon boots

Until space travel becomes more common you won't be able to obtain direct evidence of this. You can do thought experiments and make predictions to understand the situation. You should be able to find out more about the boots from reference sources, such as the NASA web site. Would the astronauts float away from the Moon's surface if they didn't wear boots?

An astronaut's airtight suit looks quite similar to the suit worn by a deep-sea diver. Deep-sea divers have heavy boots to prevent them floating up to the surface, so it is easy to assume that in the lower gravity of the Moon the astronauts need heavy boots to avoid floating away from the Moon's surface. In fact the boots are there as part of a completely airtight suit. Heavy boots are not necessary to keep the astronauts on the Moon. The boots must be as light as possible so that they don't use extra fuel at lift-off. How do you think heavy and light things behave on the Moon if you drop them?

# Energy resources and energy transfer

10

Energy resources and energy transfer

# 10.1 Wind up

You can investigate this problem using a wind-up toy. Try turning the key different numbers of times, and see how far the car travels. Don't wind it too much or the spring will break. How will you work out how fast it is going? You could use data logging equipment or a stopwatch to measure how long it takes for the car to travel a certain distance. What kind of graph could you use to find out if there is a relationship between the number of turns, the speed and the distance travelled?

Winding the spring in the wind-up car stores the energy that the car needs to help it to move. Winding the spring more will store more energy, and this should make the car go further. It should also make the car go faster. However it is hard to predict how far or how fast the car will go if you wind the spring twice as much. Did you find this? Springs often work differently as they get tighter, and each toy will be different depending on the type and size of spring and how well it is made. Some clocks use wind-up springs. How do you think they manage to keep time so well?

# 10.2 Ice cubes

You can investigate melting ice quite easily, using different sized ice cubes and timing how long they take to melt. Keep the other conditions the same. This will show whether the size makes a difference to the speed of melting. What will happen if you repeat the investigation at different temperatures? Will this make a difference to which ice cube melts first?

The bigger ice cube needs to be heated more to melt it because it has a bigger volume, so there is more ice to be melted. The bigger cube has a larger surface area, so it will gain energy more quickly from the surroundings. How fast it melts depends on the ratio between the surface area and the volume. The smaller cube has a larger surface area to volume ratio than the bigger cube, so the smaller ice cube will melt first. Using what you have found out, how long do you think a one litre block of ice will take to melt at room temperature?

# 10.3 Ice cream

You can't do a practical investigation to solve this problem, but you can probably work it out. Finding out more about what heat and cold mean will be useful. Thinking about light and dark may be helpful. What is it that could travel from your hand to the ice cream? What is it that could travel from the ice cream to your hand? What happens when you put food in a fridge? How does a cool box keep ice cream cool?

The word 'heat' can cause confusion, since it is used as both a noun and a verb in everyday language. Energy is probably a more useful word. When a substance gets hotter, its particles are moving more rapidly. This is because they have more energy. Hot objects will transfer this energy to colder objects, but cold objects can't transfer energy to hotter objects. Energy will be transferred from your hand along the spoon to the ice cream. The spoon feels cold because your hand is transferring energy along the spoon and into the ice cream. Can you explain why a wooden spoon doesn't feel as cold as a metal one?

# 10.4 Fast car

Check the fuel gauge in a car before and after a long journey. What does this show about whether fuel has been used? Where does the energy come from to make a car move? Where does the energy end up? Can you see evidence of energy being transferred?

Fuel is not energy, but it is a source of energy when it is burned with oxygen from the air. As the car travels it needs energy to make the engine work. The fuel is used in supplying energy to do this. The energy itself is not used up. It is transferred to the wheels and makes the wheels go round. The wheels and engine get hot, and this transfers energy to the environment, making the ground and air slightly warmer. The energy is not made and it is not used up − it is simply transferred from one place to another. Can you use what you have learnt to track energy transfers in other everyday situations, like a television set or mobile phone? Where does the energy come from? Where does it end up? What do you think are the most fuel-efficient ways of travelling?

Energy resources and energy transfer

# 10.5 Sunbathing

You can check each of the statements in turn. Can you see the effects of energy from the Sun? Does it heat us up, make us sunburnt, cause fires? Can you observe what makes people feel more or less energetic? Does it depend on the outside temperature, on whether they have eaten recently, on the time of day, on how much they have slept, and other factors? Do plants get energy from the Sun? Where do plants get their food from? Do they need light to survive?

This situation is confusing because we use the word energy to mean different things. Energy from the Sun is transferred to our bodies, but we can't use it directly. It makes us hotter, so our skin temperature rises and we start to sweat to cool down. When we sunbathe we feel less energetic because the warm sunshine can make us feel sleepy. We don't have less energy – we just feel less like moving, which is different. Use what you have learnt to explain why cold-blooded animals lie in the sun and how that helps them to survive.

# 10.6 Black and white car

The simplest way to find out about cars getting hotter in the Sun is to make a model. You can do this by getting two similar boxes and painting them black or white, then leaving them in the sunshine for a while. You can compare the temperatures in the two boxes by using a thermometer or temperature sensor inside each box. Does the colour make a difference to the temperature? What happens if you test other colours (green, red, blue, etc.) in the same way?

Both cars get hotter standing in the Sun because the windows let the sunlight in but prevent much of the energy from leaving (just like a greenhouse). However, black surfaces absorb more of the light from the Sun than white surfaces. This is why one surface looks black and the other white. When the energy from the sunlight is absorbed it doesn't disappear, it causes the car to get hotter. The black car absorbs more energy from the sunlight and gets hotter than the white car. It will also radiate more energy. However, in normal circumstances the temperature inside the black car will be hotter than the white car. Can you use what you have learnt to explain why it is better to have white houses in a hot climate? What do you think will be the best colour clothes to wear to keep you cool?

Energy resources and energy transfer

# 10.7 In the wind

You can find out about cooling by filling a container with hot water and using a fan to blow air over the container. Does the wind cool it down? Try wrapping the container in moist tissue paper so that the water in the tissue paper will evaporate. Does evaporation cool it down? What will the wind and evaporation do together? What difference does it make if you wrap an insulator (such as wool or bubble wrap) around the container?

The wind feels cold because it makes water evaporate faster from the surface of the skin. The wind blows away the moist air that usually surrounds our bodies, and this allows more water to evaporate, so this cools the skin. The wind also blows away the layer of warm air surrounding our bodies. The layer of warm air is replaced by colder air, so we lose energy by warming this new layer of air. This makes us colder. Can you use what you have learnt to explain why you cool down quickly when you get wet? How do you think animals can survive outside in winter?

# 10.8 In the mountains

You can't do a simple practical investigation to find out about this problem. You will have to get evidence through research. You can use books, CDs or internet web sites to find out about the relationship between altitude and temperature, and what kinds of things can affect that relationship. Is it usually hotter or colder in the mountains? Does sheltering from the wind make a difference? You can do some thought experiments too. What happens to the temperature if you go outside the Earth's atmosphere?

An insulator, like a thick coat, can hold a layer of air around our bodies, and this keeps us warm. The atmosphere is a layer of air at the Earth's surface, and this keeps the Earth warm. The layer of air traps the energy from the Sun so the Earth's surface becomes warmer. The atmosphere gets thinner (in other words, less dense) as the altitude increases. At high altitude there is less air to trap the energy from the Sun, so it gets colder. Outside the Earth's atmosphere where there is no air it is extremely cold. How do you think people who travel into space keep warm?

Energy resources and energy transfer

You can find out whether the sound accumulates in the box by using a sound sensor and data logging equipment. Turn the radio on very low, put it in the box, and see if the sound gradually gets louder. Measuring whether the temperature changes in the box is more tricky, and is complicated by the battery getting hot as the radio plays. You can find out whether vibration or movement causes objects to get warmer by drilling into a piece of wood or hitting a piece of metal with a hammer. What would happen to the light if you put a torch inside the box?

The energy transferred as sound from the radio has to go somewhere. It makes the particles in the air and in the walls of the box vibrate slightly faster, so the box will get fractionally warmer. This change in temperature is very small, so you will not be able to measure it. Can you use what you have learnt to explain how a sonic toothbrush works?

# 10.10 Kettle

You can find out about the amount of energy needed to heat up the kettle with a practical investigation. Try keeping water in a container hot for an hour, using a mini immersion heater. Compare this with a container that you heat up every 15 minutes. Which container uses most electricity? Will the size of the container make a difference? Will a hot water tank in a house act in the same way as a kettle?

It is easy to think that it takes less energy to keep a container of water constantly hot than it does to heat it up occasionally when it is needed. It doesn't. The higher the temperature of the water, the more energy it loses to the environment. If the water is constantly hot then it is constantly losing energy to the environment, so it requires more energy to keep it at that temperature. When the water is the same temperature as the surroundings it is not losing any energy, so the most energy-efficient approach is to heat it up only when it is needed. Can you use what you have learnt to think about the most energy-efficient way to heat a house?

Energy resources and energy transfer

# 10.11 Warm Sun

You can't do a simple practical investigation to find out whether the Earth is getting warmer. You can research this question using books, CDs and internet sites to find out about the Earth's temperature, what causes it to be that temperature, whether it has been that temperature for a long time, and whether its temperature is changing. As you find out more you will see a connection between scientific knowledge and personal action, and this has implications for decisions you make about your personal lifestyle. What do you think will happen if the Earth does get much warmer?

Although the Earth constantly receives energy from the Sun, it also radiates energy back into space. In this way the temperature remains in balance. There is evidence that the Earth's temperature has changed significantly in the past (such as in the 'Ice Age'), but over a long period of time it reaches an equilibrium and the overall temperature stabilises. In recent years scientists have expressed concern that the average temperature of the Earth is increasing. The increase appears small but they are concerned that it may continue to rise. Not all scientists agree about the cause and extent of the change. What evidence can you find, and how can you decide if the evidence of change is reliable or not?

# 10.12 Log fire

What is the difference between fuel and energy? Where do they come from, how do we use them, and what happens to them in a log fire? You can look these words up in books or on the internet, and discuss the ideas with your friends. You can find out more about fuel availability, renewable and non-renewable sources of energy, energy requirements and global warming. What happens to fuel and energy in your body?

Talking about the 'energy crisis' can easily cause confusion. If there is a crisis then the problem is with the availability of convenient fuels that act as stores of energy. Logs are useful for fires, but they are not very good as fuel for buses or aeroplanes. Using logs as a fuel has the advantage that they are a renewable source of energy, unlike fossil fuels (e.g. oil and coal) that take many millions of years to be replaced. Burning the logs produces carbon dioxide that can contribute to global warming, but carbon dioxide is used when new trees are grown to replace the logs that have been burnt. What arguments can you put forward about the use of different fuels in everyday life?

Energy resources and energy transfer

# References:

Alexander R. (2006) *Towards dialogic teaching.* York: Dialogos.

Black, P. and Wiliam, D. (1998) *Inside the black box.* Kings College, London.

Black, P. and Harrison, C. (2004) *Science inside the black box.* NferNelson, London.

Black, P., Harrison, C., Lee C., Marshall B. and Wiliam D. (2002) *Working inside the black box.* Kings College, London.

Keogh, B. and Naylor, S. (1999) Concept Cartoons, teaching and learning in science: an evaluation. *International Journal of Science Education,* 21 (4) 431-446.

Naylor, S. and Keogh, B. (2007) Active Assessment: thinking, learning and assessment in science. *School Science Review,* 88 (325) 73-79.

Naylor, S., Keogh, B. and Goldsworthy, A. (2004) *Active Assessment: thinking, learning and assessment in science.* Sandbach: Millgate House Publishers.

White, R. and Gunstone, R. (1992) *Probing understanding.* London: Falmer.

References

# References to research into Concept Cartoons

Chin, C. and Teou L.Y. (2009) Using Concept Cartoons in formative assessment: scaffolding students' argumentation. *International Journal of Science Education, 31, 10, 1307-1332.*

Downing, B. (2005) *Developing the nature and the role of quality argument in primary science lessons through the use of Concept Cartoons.* Unpublished PhD thesis, Manchester Metropolitan University.

Education Extra (1998) *Science on the Underground: An evaluation of the Concept Cartoon project by Education Extra.* London: Education Extra.

Ekici, F., Ekici, E. and Aydin, F. (2007) Utility of Concept Cartoons in diagnosing and overcoming misconceptions related to photosynthesis. *International Journal of Science Education, 2, 4,111-124.*

Kabapinar, F. (2005) Effectiveness of teaching via Concept Cartoons from the point of view of constructivist approach. *Educational Sciences: Theory and Practice, 5,1,135-146.*

Keogh, B. and Naylor, S. (1993) Learning in science: another way in. *Primary Science Review, 26, 22-23.*

Keogh, B. (1995) An exploration of the possible value of cartoons as a teaching approach in science. *Unpublished MA dissertation,* Manchester Metropolitan University.

Keogh, B. and Naylor, S. (1996) Learning in science: cartoons as an innovative teaching and learning approach. In K. Calhoun, R. Panwar and S. Shrum (Eds.) *Proceedings of the 8th Symposium of the International Organisation of Science and Technology Education,* Vol 3, 133-9. Edmonton, Canada.

Keogh, B. and Naylor, S. (1997) Making sense of constructivism in the classroom. *Science Teacher Education, 20, 12-14.*

Keogh, B. and Naylor, S. (1997) Developing children's ideas: putting constructivism into practice in teacher education. In R. Feasey (Ed.) *Proceedings of the third summer conference for teacher education in primary science, 139-146.* University of Durham, UK.

Keogh, B. and Naylor, S. (1998) Teaching and Learning in Science using Concept Cartoons. *Primary Science Review, 51, 14-16.*

154

Keogh B and Naylor S (1999), Concept Cartoons, teaching and learning in science: an evaluation. *International Journal of Science Education*, 21,4,431-446.

Keogh B. & Naylor S. (2000) Teaching and learning in science using Concept Cartoons: why Dennis wants to stay in at playtime. *Investigating* 16, 3, 10-14.

Keogh B. & Naylor S. (2000) Concept Cartoons and issues in science teacher education. *Proceedings of the SCIcentre/ASET conference 2000*, 108-112. Leicester.

Keogh, B., Naylor, S. and Wilson, C. (1998) Concept Cartoons: a new perspective on physics education. *Physics Education*, 33, 4, 219-224.

Kinchin, I. (2000) Concept mapping activities to help students understand photosynthesis – and teachers understand students. *School Science Review*, 82 (299), 11-14.

Millar, L. and Murdoch, J. (2002) A penny for your thoughts. Primary Science Review, 72, 26-9.

Morris, M. Merritt, M., Fairclough, S., Birrell, N. and Howitt. C. (2007) Trialling Concept Cartoons in early childhood teaching and learning of science. *Teaching Science*.

Naylor, S. and Keogh, B. (1999), Constructivism in the Classroom: Theory into Practice. *Journal of Science Teacher Education*, 10(2) 93-106.

Naylor, S. and Keogh, B. (1999), Science on the Underground: an initial evaluation. *Public Understanding of Science*, 8, 1-18.

Naylor S. and Keogh B. (2000) *Concept Cartoons in Science Education*. Sandbach: Millgate House Publishers.

Naylor, S., Keogh, B., de Boo, M. and Feasey, R. (2000) Researching formative assessment: Concept Cartoons as an auditing strategy. In R.Duit (Ed.) *Research in Science Education: Past, Present and Future*. Dordrecht: Kluwer.

Naylor S. and Keogh B. (2002) Concept Cartoons. *Teaching thinking*, 9, 8-12.

Naylor S., Keogh B. and Downing, B. (2003) Argumentation in the primary science classroom. *Science Teacher Education*, 35, 3-5.

Naylor S., Keogh B. and Downing, B. (2007) Argumentation and primary science. *Research in Science Education*, 37, 17-39.

Oluk, S. and Ozalp, I. (2007) The teaching of global environmental problems according to the constructivist approach: as a focal point of the problem and the availability of Concept Cartoons. *Educational Sciences Theory and Practice*, 7, 2, 881-896.

Rahmat, F. A. (2009). Use of Concept Cartoons as a strategy to address pupils' misconceptions in primary four science topic on matter. In A. L. Tan, H. M. Wong, & S., Tan (Eds.), *Action research: Empowering my practice in teaching science* (pp. 11-37). Singapore: National Institute of Education and Science Exploria, East Zone Centre of Excellence for Primary Science.

Stephenson P. and Warwick P. (2002) Using Concept Cartoons to support progression in students' understanding of light. *Physics Education*, 37, 2, 135-141.

# Concept Cartoon and Active Assessment publications

Dabell, J. (2006) *Thinking about maths* poster set. Sandbach: Millgate House Publishers.

Dabell, J., Keogh, B. and Naylor, S. (2008) *Concept Cartoons in mathematics education.* Sandbach: Millgate House Publishers.

Keogh, B. and Naylor, S. (1997) *Starting points for science.* Sandbach: Millgate House Publishers.

Keogh, B. and Naylor, S. (1997) *Thinking about science* poster set. Sandbach: Millgate House Publishers.

Keogh, B. and Naylor, S. (1999) *Thinking about science 2* poster set. Sandbach: Millgate House Publishers.

Keogh, B., Dabell, J. and Naylor, S. (2008) *Active Assessment: thinking, learning and assessment in English.* Sandbach: Millgate House Publishers.

Keogh, B., Dabell, J. and Naylor, S. (2010) *Active Assessment: thinking, learning and assessment in mathematics.* Sandbach: Millgate House Publishers.

Keogh, B. & Naylor, S. (2006, 2007) Spellbound Science 1 and 2. Millgate House Publishers.

Naylor, S. and Keogh, B. (2000) *Concept Cartoons in science education.* Sandbach: Millgate House Publishers.

Naylor, S., Keogh, B. and Goldsworthy, A. (2004) *Active Assessment: thinking, learning and assessment in science.* Sandbach: Millgate House Publishers.

Naylor, S. and Naylor, B. (2000) *Science Questions books series.* London, Hodder Children's Books. Now available from Millgate House Publishers. Published by Millgate House Publishers on CD ROM (2009)

References